ELON MUSK'S

BILLIONAIRE SCHOOL

ELON MUSK'S

BILLIONAIRE SCHOOL

Easy Lessons for Galactic Domination

Rob Sears

CANONGATE

First published in Great Britain, the USA and Canada in 2022
by Canongate Books Ltd, 14 High Street, Edinburgh EH1 1TE

Distributed in the USA by Publishers Group West
and in Canada by Publishers Group Canada

canongate.co.uk

1

British Library Cataloguing-in-Publication Data
A catalogue record for this book is available on
request from the British Library

ISBN 978 1 83885 947 3

Typeset in Archer by Palimpsest Book Production Ltd,
Falkirk, Stirlingshire

Printed and bound in Great Britain by Clays Ltd, Elcograf S.p.A.

MIX
Paper from
responsible sources
FSC
www.fsc.org   FSC® C018072

Welcome to Billionaire School

Most business schools promise an enriching experience, but not many can guarantee that their students will soon be among the world's wealthiest people.

Elon Musk's Billionaire School is different because the tips and home exercises in our curriculum are based on the proven strategies of today's richest and most visionary tech billionaires, including Elon Musk himself.

That means we can guarantee* you a ten-figure net worth and at least one admiring profile piece in a major newspaper within thirty days of completing our course.

You're on the verge of the super-rich life of your dreams. Picture it: you'll be running either 69 or 420 different major tech companies at once. Your

---

* Not a guarantee. See lesson 16, 'Promise the moon'.

inventions will be so smart they'll invent more inventions. Every single one of your 'shower thoughts' will spawn new industries, currencies, branches of law . . .

Some readers may be sceptical that we can really deliver on these fantastic claims. To remove any doubt, we'd like to share a few of the Frequently Asked Questions we sometimes get from prospective billionaires during our open days, along with our responses.

Q: How could a few lessons possibly make me a billionaire?

You should believe in yourself more! Just by opening this book you've demonstrated a proactive attitude to wealth accumulation. In fact, give or take $500 million, you're halfway there already.

Let us try to lay out how straightforward it can be using a chart that many of our students find helpful.

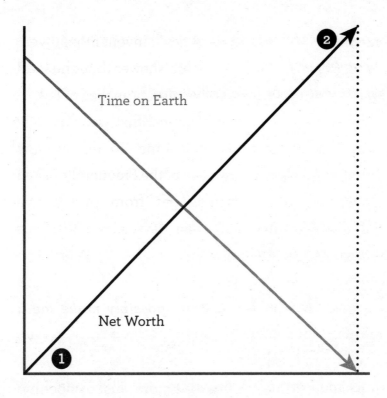

Time on Earth

Net Worth

You are currently at point 1 on the graph – you might not have much money but, all being well, you've plenty of time ahead of you. If you're young, you might even be a 'time billionaire', with over a billion seconds left to spend however you please! All you have to do now is convert your remaining time on earth into dollars at a sufficiently quick rate that you can reach your target 'WAD' (wealth at death) before you become 'time bankrupt' and expire (point 2).

Success is that easy!

Q: I've heard that Elon Musk had a privileged upbringing. What if I don't have the right background or education to be a billionaire?

It is true that many billionaires fit quite a narrow demographic. Musk is one of nine white men in the world's top ten richest people according to *Forbes*.[1] His father owned properties stately enough to be rented out as embassies,[2] as well as a stake in an emerald mine in Zambia.[3]

However, the Billionaire School is working to ensure that tomorrow's extreme inequality is more diverse and inclusive. We offer grants, scholarships and mentoring programmes for both non-white and female candidates who have demonstrated a genuine interest in becoming billionaires (i.e. an accumulated net worth of $50 million or more).

Q: I don't have any money. I've got family responsibilities and a job I can't afford to leave. How do I even get started?

Please note that we also offer hardship bursaries. To apply, simply find our stand in the VIP section at the Davos conference.

Even if you don't receive a bursary, consider what really matters in life. Your family might not see you so often, but wouldn't they be happy if you came home one day with a billion dollars and an electric nanny?

As for your regular-paying job, you may not actually have to leave it. With hard work, anyone can accumulate a billion dollars. You'll just have to be prepared to work weekends and take on overtime. And continue doing so for 15,000 years.

Admittedly, founding your own start-up might be a more practical route.

Q: What is your school's connection with Elon Musk?

The Billionaire School is not officially endorsed by Elon Musk, as he has not replied to our emails, but his influence on our teaching and philosophy cannot be overstated. To us, he represents the pinnacle of what a billionaire can be. Not only does he have the most, he also gives the most, sharing with the world his technologies, his considered views on the issues of the day, his optimism for humanity's multi-planetary future and his potent genetic material.

We also admire and have much to learn from other well-known tech billionaires. Amazon founder Jeff Bezos's willingness back in the nineties to take on the evil might of independent bookstores, for example, remains an inspiration to us all. So too does the rise of youthful Meta boss Mark Zuckerberg. We can learn much from his healthy acquisitive appetite (ninety-four companies bought so far) and his unconventional and free-spirited decision not to create his own space programme, but travel into the metaverse instead.*

Q: *If all this was really as easy as you claim, wouldn't everyone be a billionaire?*

Being a billionaire has come to be regarded as something that's somehow 'elite', 'exclusive' or 'out of reach' – but that couldn't be further from the truth. If you spend time with billionaires – in their private jets or while they're getting blood transfusions from

---

* Beyond the tech world, we are also inspired by non-tech tycoons such as old-school French fashion magnate, Bernard Arnault, who has been #1 richest person as recently as 2021 but otherwise stays out of the limelight (he has a fortieth as many Google hits as Musk). Or #59, billionaire Qin Yinglin, with his pig-breeding empire. Although our school draws chiefly on the examples of high-profile tech billionaires, we believe the principles we teach can help students dominate any industry they choose.

young donors, for instance[4] – you'll find they are just like us. The only difference is that they've worked harder and smarter.

Today, the lives of the tech billionaires are public. Anybody can follow their example and emulate what they have – and if you don't, you only have yourself to blame. In fact, we would go further: billionaires are the people saving our world, so if you're not rich, or at least intent on getting rich, you're not a good person.

At the Billionaire School we believe everyone should be focused on building their personal asset base, through any means possible. Yes, your path to wealth may require you to build a demonic AI, or ravage the environment and exacerbate climate change – but it's only through the money you make that you can also hope to solve the terrifying problems you have created.

That's why – if you want to be a billionaire – there's nothing we'd find more enriching than to teach you.

Visualising your goal

To help you decide on a personal financial goal and track your progress as you work through this book, we've created the visualisation tool opposite.

The size of the large rectangle represents Elon Musk's net worth at the time of going to press. To become an entry-level billionaire, however, you need only accumulate assets equivalent to the tiny rectangle at the top left. Looks pretty easy, right? If so, perhaps you'd like to set a more ambitious stretch goal. (We've added some other rectangles to the chart to help put these big numbers in perspective.)

Why not draw a box representing your objective and pin this page somewhere prominent in your home? That way, every time you walk past, you can stare at your box, softly cackle, and remind yourself of the money that's coming your way.

☐ = $1 billion

Elon Musk's net worth (about $260 billion)

☐ This much ($180 million) would be enough to fill a paddling pool with pure gold coins and dive in like Scrooge McDuck (don't do this, the injuries could be horrific)

Combined production budget of last ten Marvel movies (around $2 billion). This would be enough to make your own Marvel Cinematic Parallel Universe only you and your houseguests would get to watch.

One year's salary for all NBA players (around $4 billion). With this much, you could stage the entire league in your basement.

According to the head of the World Food Bank, this ($6 billion) would be enough to prevent geopolitical instability, mass migration and save 42 million people on the brink of starvation

The most advanced state-of-the-art nuclear-powered aircraft carrier costs about this much ($13 billion). Could be handy if your private jet collection gets too big to keep at home, as well as helping you deal with rivals.

This – $21 billion – is equivalent to the Gross Domestic Product of Trinidad & Tobago. A good amount to aim for if you want to be taken as seriously as a small country.

Sources in endnotes[1]

Unit 1

STARTING OUT

Savour this moment. You and your net worth are about to go on a beautiful journey together. Who knows how high you'll climb?

It's exciting – but before you get ahead of yourself, you need to lay some foundations. This unit covers basic billionaire principles and lessons from Musk's early life. They say the first million is the hardest, so don't feel bad if it takes several days – or even weeks! – to hit the seven-figure mark. When you're starting out and money is tight, managing your finances and cutting down on little treats can make all the difference. The savings from simply refraining from eating Mexico's entire avocado supply for twelve months, for instance, could put you on next year's rich lists.

Visualise your take-off. You've got this!

Lesson 1

Don't delay another moment

Once you become a billionaire, your life will be packed with incredible experiences and deeds. In other words, you owe it to humanity and yourself to hurry up and start getting rich.

Even as a child, Elon Musk made the most of every moment. At four, he was telling people he wanted to be a millionaire.[1] At eleven, dressed in a suit and tie, he was bombarding professors with questions at a computing conference in Johannesburg.[2] And by twelve, he'd already sold the code for his video game Blastar to a magazine for $500.[3]

That same sense of urgency still drives Musk today: he even pees quickly ('It's like a fire hose,' a colleague claims[4]), and wolfs down food and drink in meetings. 'If there was a way that I could not eat, so I could work more, I would not eat,' Musk has mused. 'I wish there was a way to get nutrients without sitting down for a meal.'[5]

You may not have started life with the same urgency as Musk, but don't panic. You'll be on the billionaire track in no time, just as long as you significantly speed up your bodily functions and optimise the time you waste on unproductive activities like rest.

TRY AT HOME

Because Musk believes in an even more fantastic future, he makes the most of every moment even now. See if you can find an ounce of fat on this example day from his schedule. (Hint: you won't be able to.)

A typical day in Elon Musk's schedule. Not a second is wasted.

Monday 27

00:00 – 03:30	Sleeping
04:00	Tweeting
05:00	Sleeping
06:00	Tweeting
07:00	Breakfast and tweeting
08:00	Factory walkaround and tweeting
09:00	Toilet break and tweeting
10:00	Shitposting
11:00	Photo with dictator and tweeting
12:00	Falcon 9 launch and tweeting
13:00	Working lunch and tweeting
14:00	Shitposting and AGM
16:00	Attorney briefing and tweeting
18:00	Write all staffer praising team's hard work
19:00	Tweeting about lazy staff
20:00	Flight home in private jet and tweeting
21:00	Wind down at home with a quick Twitter session
22:00	Fall asleep at factory
23:00	Tweeting

Go where the growth is

With the right attitude, someone like you could probably become a billionaire in a locked room. But migrating towards money will make your future success even more of a sure thing.

Musk had always idealised North America as the land where dreams come true, and he made his way there at the age of seventeen, working at relatives' farms and lumber mills for a while before figuring out his destiny. You'll want to be similarly prepared to wash plates for a few months before you completely upend your new country's economic and industrial systems.

Musk timed his arrival in the US well, just as the internet was taking shape and nerdy entrepreneurs were taking over the economy. In California at the time, money was being thrown at anyone who could make a website and dazzle investors. Musk exhibited an early talent for showmanship when he disguised his standard PC inside a massive plastic box on wheels, so it appeared to the clueless as though his rudimentary early business ideas were running on a supercomputer.[6]

TIP FROM THE TOP

Before jumping on a plane to maximise your chances of riches, consider the stats. In 2022, the countries minting the most new billionaires were China (with sixty-two new billionaires), the USA (fifty) and India (twenty-nine).[7] These countries can be funny about handing out visas to entrepreneurs like you, so be ready to wow any sceptical border guards with a jazzy pitch deck.

Lesson 3

Head off on a road trip

Need an idea for your first proper business venture? A formative road trip is a sure-fire way to get inspired. Simply give yourself up to the rhythms of the open highway, and by the time you've crossed the country, the smell of taco wrappers in a hot car will have almost certainly baked a path to global domination into your neurons.

It was on a journey across the US to California, in a '70s BMW, that Musk and his brother Kimbal brainstormed the idea for their first big success – an online city guide called Zip2.[8] Musk's renewable energy company SolarCity was founded on another such trip in an RV with some of his cousins.[9] And it was on yet another seaboard-to-seaboard drive, from New York to Seattle in an '87 Chevy, that Jeff and Mackenzie Bezos came up with the business plan for Amazon.[10]

Remember, your road trip will become part of the origin story for the intergalactic trading dynasty over which you'll one day preside. So make sure to take pictures.

TIP FROM THE TOP

If you decide to follow in the tyre tracks of the billionaires, don't miss these inspirational roadside stops:

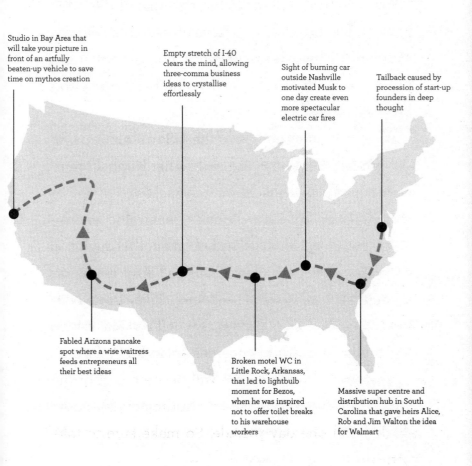

Studio in Bay Area that will take your picture in front of an artfully beaten-up vehicle to save time on mythos creation

Empty stretch of I-40 clears the mind, allowing three-comma business ideas to crystallise effortlessly

Sight of burning car outside Nashville motivated Musk to one day create even more spectacular electric car fires

Tailback caused by procession of start-up founders in deep thought

Fabled Arizona pancake spot where a wise waitress feeds entrepreneurs all their best ideas

Broken motel WC in Little Rock, Arkansas, that led to lightbulb moment for Bezos, when he was inspired not to offer toilet breaks to his warehouse workers

Massive super centre and distribution hub in South Carolina that gave heirs Alice, Rob and Jim Walton the idea for Walmart

Lesson 4

Drop out of college

When starting out, you'll want to show investors that you're not just smart but passionate – maybe even to the point of being willing to ritually disembowel yourself in their offices. 'My mentality is that of a samurai. I would rather commit seppuku than fail,' Musk (a sword owner) reportedly told an early investor in his first company.[11]

A less extreme way to demonstrate your conviction is to drop out of the most prestigious college that will have you, as Musk did when he quit his Stanford PhD after forty-eight hours. Breezing through the quad and straight out again in this manner has become an expected beat in the first act of many super-rich founders: the list of other billionaire dropouts includes Bill Gates, Mark Zuckerberg, Steve Jobs, Larry Page, Larry Ellison (Oracle) and Jack Dorsey (Twitter).

It's even been estimated that, due to the skewing effects of Gates's and Zuckerberg's wealth, those who drop out of Harvard make more money on average than those who graduate.

TIP FROM THE TOP

If you have already completed a course of further education, it could be hard to convince investors you're serious about your business idea. If you find yourself in this situation, one solution would be to loudly quit something else prestigious instead: a budding career as a pop star or professional athlete, for example. If that's not possible, burn your college transcripts, destroy any record of your graduation, and deny everything.

Lesson 5

Stay up late with your start-up crew

Whether your first business is destined to be a stepping stone to bigger things (like Musk's Zip2) or the basis of your fortune (like Bezos's Amazon and Zuckerberg's Facebook), a young start-up can be demanding at first. Fortunately, that's also when businesses are at their most adorable. They're so idealistic at that age!

In the early days, Musk was happy to stay up tending to Zip2 each night, finally falling asleep at the office on a bean bag beside his desk. The first coder in the next morning was expected to wake him with a kick, as if Musk was a dog with some knowledge of C++.[12] Then he'd go right back to work.

'Work hard every waking hour,' Musk says. 'If you do the simple math, say if somebody else is working fifty hours [a week] and you're working one hundred, you'll get twice [as much] done in the course of a year as the other company.'

TIP FROM THE **TOP**

The early lives of the tech billionaires are full of stories of all-night coding sessions, like Mark Zuckerberg's famous Red Bull-fuelled hackathons in the early days of Facebook.[13] If you can't code, don't worry, just stay up 24/7 hammering at your keyboard and muttering things like 'This system's got more bugs than a bait store' and 'I must have put a decimal point in the wrong place'. With a bit of luck, your team will never guess your secret.

Lesson 6

Consume a lot of sci-fi

To lead your business – and one day the world – to new heights, you need a vision of the future. Fortunately, ready-made ones are available in the science fiction section at the library. All you have to do is issue instructions such as 'Build this' a few times in the margins of a book with an alien citadel on the cover, then toss it in the direction of your engineering team.

Sci-fi is undoubtedly Silicon Valley's favourite genre and has captured the fantasies of many young tech billionaires. Its influence on Elon Musk can be seen everywhere, from the alphanumeric codes used instead of his kids' names (his sixth son for instance is called X Æ A-12) to his drone ships being named after spacecraft in Iain M. Banks space operas[14] (examples include *Just Read the Instructions* and *Of Course I Still Love You*). He's been known to talk at length about the feasibility of *Star Wars*-style ray-guns based on ultracapacitors.[15]

Fellow sci-fi-loving space tycoon Jeff Bezos has

looked to sci-fi not just for ideas but personnel. He turned *Star Trek* actor William Shatner into a real-life astronaut[16] and hired cult novelist Neal Stephenson to come up with out-of-the-box new spacecraft concepts[17] (presumably as part of Bezos's long-held ambition to offer Amazon Prime deliveries to Pluto).

TIP FROM THE TOP

When in need of product ideas, raid the work of sci-fi authors from Robert Heinlein to Octavia Butler – they are our most brilliant and visionary futurists. Just ignore any subtext you might notice about capitalistic hubris; the people who write these things make up stories for a living and can be complete airheads.

Be the alpha

If you like to be in control of everything, good news – it's one more way in which you and Elon Musk are alike.

According to a co-worker's account, meetings with Musk go better if employees position themselves at a lower height than him, so he is looking down on them.[18] He is also known to demand hour-by-hour – sometimes minute-by-minute – plans of how they will solve a problem,[19] and insists on controlling details down to which acronyms are permitted for use in his companies (because 'ASS' – Acronyms Seriously Suck).[20]

Musk also has a reputation for setting impossible deadlines for his team, knocking them off balance so they have to work nonstop even to deliver late[21] (perhaps one of the reasons his colleagues eventually ousted him as CEO of Zip2, and later of PayPal as well).

Musk's first wife Justine says that, on their wedding day, he told her: 'I'm the alpha in this relationship.'

One way this view apparently manifested itself was in asking her to dye her hair lighter and lighter shades of blonde.[22] Colleagues, quoted anonymously in a *Wall Street Journal* article, even claimed that Musk's mood fluctuated according to how blonde she became.[23]

TRY AT HOME

The greater your dominant streak, the greater your chances of keeping control of a vast equity and cryptocurrency fortune. Find out if you're alpha enough with the exercise overleaf.

How alpha are you?

To assess your alpha billionaire tendencies, simply decide how much you agree with each of these statements and add up your results to get your score.

I am comfortable giving orders.
Strongly disagree   Strongly agree

1   2   3   4   5

I always know what I want.

1   2   3   4   5

I shouldn't have to explain my reasoning. Ever.

1   2   3   4   5

I always sit at the head of the table and eat first.

1   2   3   4   5

Other people don't know their own minds.

1   2   3   4   5

Before every meeting, I souse the chairs with my powerful natural pheromones.

1   2   3   4   5

Scores

6–20

You may be smart, but you have a tendency to let others trample over you. Practise taking control – perhaps start with a custom coffee order and slowly work up to striking terror into your employees.

21–30

You have a few alpha traits! You usually get your own way – but you'll need to stay on guard if you want to keep an iron grip on your business empire.

Refused to answer the questions because you never let anyone else tell you what to do

The true alpha, able to impose your will and arbitrary preferences on any situation. Born to be a tech boss.

Lesson 8

Splash out on something

So you've followed the lessons so far and you're making some serious money! Congratulations. You should make a big-ticket purchase to see how it feels and make your debut as a Very Rich Person.

When Musk sold Zip2 and became not wealthy but insanely wealthy for the first time, he bought his dream car, a $1m McLaren F1, and invited CNN to film it being delivered. Still trying on his ultra-rich-guy persona at the time, he came out with a string of zingers such as 'Cash is cash. That is just a very large number of Benjamin Franklins' and confidently told viewers that his next company would likely be a 'multi-billion-dollar bonanza'.[24]

Later, Musk showed off the car to Peter Thiel (a PayPal co-founder). 'Watch this,' Musk said, and gunned the McLaren's gold-plated engine so hard the car hit an embankment and flipped into the air. Glass shattered, tyres burst . . . but the two men's lucky streak continued: they crawled out and hitch-hiked to their next meeting.[25]

TRY ᴬᵀ HOME

As a newly minted rich person, you'll be keen to splash out on something. But before you do, consider what your first big purchase will say about the kind of billionaire you're going to be . . .

Purchase	What it says about you
Island with dormant volcano	Definitely on track to be a supervillain
One-of-a-kind sports car with 300mph top speed	Willing to risk safety of self, pedestrians and the economy
Fabergé egg to display at home	Interested in meeting a diverse group of new friends with elaborate heist-planning skills
Huge solar yacht	Responsibly preparing for climate crisis and its impact on dick-waving contests
Momma's dream house	You really love your momma. Sweet!
Deluxe New Zealand bunker	Not panicking, you just appreciate the natural beauty of lead walls
Sourdough from that really nice café	Taking your relationship with money one step at a time

Unit 2

MILLIONS TO BILLIONS

This is your maximum growth phase – when you'll go from being one of the haves to one of the have-yachts. And it's going to be maximum fun.

At some point during the lessons in this unit, your net worth will pass the crucial one-billion-dollar milestone. But don't stop now! Frame your first billion, hang it on the wall as a reminder of where you came from, and keep going.

Remember that there are many more mountains to be conquered, like Olympus Mons, the highest point on Mars. You don't want to be retiring to a mansion that's not the biggest around and getting a tight feeling in your tummy every time a stetson-wearing tourist makes it into space without you. And how hard would it suck if the first asteroid-mining trillionaire isn't you?

Avoid these awful fates by focusing on growth, growth and more growth. You can sit back and enjoy it later (just kidding, there is no logical endpoint).

Lesson 9

Find a new field to disrupt

If you've sold a business and made a large profit, it's time to look for a new industry to disrupt.

This was Musk's position after the sale of Zip2 in 1999. He didn't know much about banking but launched online bank X.com on the hunch that bankers were too complacent to change with the times (a bet that paid off when X.com merged with PayPal and later sold to eBay, netting Musk $180 million).[1]

Jeff Bezos is another master at shaking up an established field. When he began Amazon as an online bookstore, it wasn't because he liked books or knew much about them. Rather, Bezos had identified them as the niche most easily disrupted by ecommerce tech (then in its early days). Books, he explained in a TV interview,[2] were cuboid objects that were simple to store, ship and sell. They came in an endless variety. And you could fit a wider range in a Delaware fulfilment centre than a bookstore could ever hope to offer.

Bezos didn't need to read any books to conclude that – of all the opportunities on earth – bookselling was the one that would give his business the most explosive start.

Keep your strategic horizons broad by subscribing to a wide range of trade magazines, such as *Moth Sexing International*, *Modern Arc Welder* or *Pyjama Dispatch*. Pay special attention to the industries you're least interested in, as these are the ones you'll be able to exploit most dispassionately.

Lesson 10

Play the probabilities

You're in the big leagues now. It's billions or bust, and that means you can shed your cautious attitude to risk and start betting on longshots.

Musk once said he thought he had a sub-10 per cent chance of getting a SpaceX craft into orbit or making a success of Tesla, but added, 'As God is my bloody witness, I am hell-bent on making it work.'[3] (A good potential audition speech if you ever decide to give up your billionaire dreams and become an actor instead.)

Jeff Bezos, similarly, claims he gave Amazon a 30 per cent chance of becoming a profitable company when he set it up. He told his parents – who gave their son $245,573 to help build the business in 1995 – that it was 'very likely they'll lose their entire investment in the company'.[4] Happy Thanksgivings were definitely at stake. The flip side was that when it took off, the value of his parents' shares rose to $30 billion, something the whole family could be thankful for.

TIP FROM THE TOP

Don't be afraid of projects with a high possibility of failure, just as long as the possible upside is immense. You should be aiming for the 'target zone' on the diagram to the right. 'It's very hard and we could get filthy rich' is okay. 'It's very hard and also there's no money in it' is something you don't often hear a billionaire say.

Potential profit ($)

Time travel

Quest for the
philosopher's stone

**TARGET
ZONE**   Artificial intelligence

Colonising Mars

Inheriting billions
(for sure the easiest
method if you're
from the right
family)

Fusion power

Cryogenics

Electric vehicles

Space travel

Hedge funds

Cloud and
e-commerce

Winning the lottery
every single week for
five years (lucky you,
but it still won't get
you over the billion
mark)

Crime/crypto empire

Sports gambling

Working a regular
job like the other
suckers

Searching for spiritual
enlightenment

Staying in bed

Chances of failure

Lesson 11

Have a fallback plan

It's not something most self-respecting billionaires want to think about, but with the long odds you face, your giant new business ventures could easily crash and burn before they take off. So you may want to get a plan B lined up in advance.

In 2016, Tesla was in serious trouble and struggling to get the Model 3 off the production line. According to a recent book,[5] Musk and Tim Cook, head of Apple, had a call about the possibility of Apple buying Tesla to prevent it from going under.

Musk was apparently interested in the idea in principle, but with one condition: he would be CEO. Sure, said Cook. (When Apple bought Beats in 2014, it kept on the founders, Jimmy Iovine and Dr. Dre, and this seemed like a similar case.)

'No,' Musk clarified. 'Apple. Apple CEO.'

'F— you,' Cook said and hung up.

TIP FROM THE **TOP**

Musk disputes this account,[6] but regardless, it's a good idea for you to have a backup plan in case of disaster. Bear in mind, this is a plan for a worst-case scenario, so be sure to choose something humble and realistic, such as chief executive of the world's biggest and most profitable tech company.

Lesson 12

Find your massive messianic mission(s)

To inspire investors to add several more zeros to your already large net worth, it helps to have an elaborate world-saving mission.

Let's consider the mission statements of three of Musk's ventures:

Tesla: 'To create the most compelling car company of the twenty-first century by driving the world's transition to electric vehicles.'

SpaceX: 'To revolutionise space technology with the ultimate goal of enabling people to live on other planets.'

OpenAI: 'To ensure that Artificial General Intelligence benefits all of humanity.'

What will your mission be? Does it sound almost impossibly ambitious? If not, think again. (Few things are worse for business than accomplishing your mission and then having nothing left to do.)

Once you've settled on the one mission that will give your company purpose and get you and your team out of bed each day, think of a few more missions. To make it to the top of the billionaire charts, you're probably going to need a bunch of these.

TRY AT HOME

Struggling to think up missions for your new ventures? Try picking-and-mixing from the options on the next page.

[My business name exists] to

pioneer quantum computing

revolutionise haircare

change the clowning industry forever

terraform Wales

open up the earth's core for tourism

enhance the productivity of toddlers

using

the blockchain   planet-cloning technology

sentient AI superyachts   midi-chlorians

huntable, plant-based game animals

narrative improv

with the ultimate aim of

saving humankind

stopping alien invasions

stopping climate change and also
causing more climate change

ending suffering and inducing
perpetual orgasm for all

finding the highest prime number

finding all the lost socks

preventing the eventual heat
death of the universe

Lesson 13

Embrace your eccentricity

To build a business with a crazy valuation from scratch, you may need a crazy-seeming business idea. This is the time to let your freak flag fly in the form of a venture so left-field it just might work.

In 2001, Musk – possibly still delirious after a severe bout of malaria – became preoccupied with space.[7] Friends worried about his mental state. One initially assumed that Musk, who'd built nothing more than websites at this point in his life, must be talking about commercial real estate. Of course, he wasn't. Rolling in money and looking for a new mission, he'd become convinced of the need to get the masses inspired about space travel again, which he would accomplish by sending mice to Mars. They'd procreate on the long journey and interested viewers would be able to watch them mating on live feeds.

As he cast around for experts willing to take his money and help him with his idiosyncratic project, Musk even travelled to Moscow with a jet scientist and a concerned college friend to purchase a couple of ICBMs (the long-range Cold War missiles that can be fitted with nuclear warheads). 'Young boy. No,' the Russian sellers told him; so he went home to set up SpaceX.[8]

TIP FROM THE TOP

If you're plagued by intrusive visions of sending mousetronauts into space inside a Russian nuke, or something else equally disturbing, you're either crazy or a genius. Check your bank balance to find out which.

Lesson 14

Take up space

Those who manage to multiply their billions are usually unafraid to take up space. That means adopting assertive body language and voicing strident opinions, as well as launching hundreds of satellites into near-Earth orbit, causing space stations to have to swerve out of their way.

At least that's what Musk has done with his Starlink fleet. So far he's shot over 2,000 satellites up there, which are now sailing around the planet at velocities of 7 km a second.[9] (A further 40,000 satellites are planned over the next few decades, creating a shell around Earth that some have speculated may alert distant aliens to our presence.[10])

This high-speed motocross event, happening 500 km above our heads, has incurred an official complaint from Beijing, which claims it had to hurriedly move the Chinese Space Station to avoid the risk of a catastrophic direct hit from one of the quarter-tonne machines.[11]

Diplomatic incidents aside, critics say Musk's

billionaire-spreading behaviour has allowed him to cement his domination of space by literally cluttering up the place so much there's no room for rival satellites.

TIP FROM THE TOP

Occupying 'unclaimed' territories of one kind or another has a rich history dating back to colonial times, from grabbing land to monopolising railroad and telegraph networks. So what kind of space will you expand into? Musk has taken up most of the thermosphere, but perhaps you could buy up orbital slots in the metaverse version of space, or obtain a monopoly on nature via genome patents. Either way, you'll want to act big and act now.

Lesson 15

Unveil early

Once you've developed some cool technology, it's time to demonstrate it to the world. Okay, the prototype is 'not ready'. Sure, it 'doesn't always work'. And true, it 'destroys the sanity and hearing of everyone in a six-mile radius'. But the investing public is clamouring for a peek and one way or another you're going to give it to them.

Musk has frequently engaged in frenetic last-minute fixes before coolly strolling onto the stage and doing his mumbling showman act. The Tesla Model S he revealed, for instance, was reportedly held together with magnets.[12] The prototype Cybertruck's bulletproof windows broke during a public demo of their strength.[13] And the first unveiling of a SolarCity Solar Roof was reportedly just an unveiling of a very ordinary roof, since the solar shingles weren't ready yet.[14]

So fear not: the rough edges of your technology can be smoothed out later. Unveiling early gets you pre-orders and liquidity, boosts the share price and lets you show the world what you've been working on. In fact, you may be able to get pretty much everything you want without selling a product at all.

TRY AT HOME

The day of an unveiling seldom goes smoothly. If one of your engineers is babbling about a problem, take a moment to admire their courage in being so candid about the issue, then fire them for negativity and find another engineer to fix it.

The following exercise will help you prepare for any last-minute prototype problems you may face.

How would you deal with these last-minute prototype problems?

Last-minute problem	Temporary repair method
Android giggling uncontrollably	Masking tape
Smart glasses look dumb	Release hallucinogen into audience
Power to cryo chamber went off and historical figures starting to smell	Send someone out to buy a Ford Lightning
Flying train just gone	Hope no one notices
Supposedly brain-enhanced pig keeps making spelling errors	Get a bunch of factory staff to run around in a crocodile making phut-phut-phut noises
Nanoswarm turned stage to dust	Own up to the mistake while disguised as a different billionaire
Terraforming efforts eight million years behind schedule	A spritz of air freshener should sort it

Lesson 16

Promise the moon

If your public wants something, your job as a billion-aire couldn't be easier: tell them they can have it, and soon!

True, it's unlikely the tech will be ready for public release next week, given the prototype burst into green flames as soon as the unveiling was over and you fired everyone involved – but since when was it a crime to be optimistic?*

Musk has a reputation for promising extremely hopeful timelines for commercialising his compa-nies' incredible inventions. Every year since 2014, for example, he's said Full Self-Driving and robotaxis were nearly ready to go mainstream. They'd be here in three months, six months . . . 'Next year, for sure, we will have over a million robotaxis on the road,' said Musk in 2019.[16] At time of writing, however, Tesla drivers still need to keep their hands hovering near the wheel, in case their car randomly brakes or

---

* Actually, being optimistic may land you in some legal trouble. A German court has ruled that Tesla's self-driving promises were misleading, and an Albuquerque driver is suing Tesla for touting features it can't deliver.[15]

mistakes an aeroplane for its mother and rushes over for a disastrous hug.[17]

Setting timelines this keen helps keep customers excited and puts a healthy pressure on your engineers. But be careful. If you can't deliver on most of your promises, people will become disillusioned – so keep making more, to ensure that only a fraction of your promises are broken at any one time.

TIP FROM THE TOP

If you're making a public promise about your products, always keep your fingers crossed behind your back. Get an underling to secretly take photos: they might prove vital later as part of a legal defence.

Lesson 17

Automate everything

Once you've got a few killer products to sell and waiting lists are full, you'll eventually have to step up your mass production capabilities. But how will you make enough units at low enough cost to justify your sky-high valuation?

Musk and Tesla's answer is twofold. The first strategy is to swallow the supply chain, making components in-house that other manufacturers buy in, such as seats. That means Tesla can keep more margin for itself.

The second answer is the 'unstoppable alien dreadnought', Musk's phrase for his vision of a totally automated factory. He's explained it as the 'machine that builds the machine', the idea being that the factory will one day be able to run by itself, with humans involved only for building it in the first place and maintenance.[18] Cars will be robo-assembled in the alien dreadnought without ever knowing a human's touch, drive out all by themselves, and be utterly shocked to meet the hairy, fleshy creatures who are supposedly in charge.

TIP FROM THE **TOP**

Why not see if you could go one further than Musk, and make the 'machine that makes the machine that makes the machine' – an autonomous factory factory that trundles around the planet, blurping out 12-square-kilometre factories in its wake until all land mass is covered in factory and, at last, it can plonk itself down for retirement on the last remaining beach? It sounds like an abject dystopia, but so do some of the best business plans, so maybe it's worth considering.

Lesson 18

Create an ecosystem

Billionaire-created ecosystems are great for everyone. Your customers are saved the trouble of even having to know about your rivals' products. You get friction-free cross-selling and a built-in fan base for everything you do.

Musk's still-developing ecosystem sees loyal consumers harvesting energy with a Tesla Solar Roof, storing it with a Tesla Solar Wall and using it to power their Tesla vehicles (while perhaps getting their internet from Starlink satellites). One day they might also summon their cars through the power of thought via his Neuralink chips, travel through his Boring Company tunnels and fly on his SpaceX spacecraft, promising 30-minute journey times to anywhere in the world.[19]

Bezos's Amazon ecosystem is of course a universal bazaar, designed to be so convenient that only customers with superhuman self-control and contrarian natures can find it in themselves to shop elsewhere.

But perhaps it's Zuckerberg whose ecosystem approach is the most shrewd. By acquiring so many different brands, he's built a tangled web. Customers may leave one part, while unknowingly continuing to use another (like many who've left Facebook, but continue to use WhatsApp).

TIP FROM THE TOP

Consider how you're going to get people through the turnstile of your ecosystem, cajole them into staying and – if they do manage to get out – trick them into re-entering through a different door. Perhaps the ideal situation is an ecosystem where you control the air supply and only means of physical escape? (See lesson 43, 'Choose a backup planet'.)

Reveal your cunning scheme

Smart billionaires think ten steps ahead. And the really smart ones, like you, make their long-range strategies public, letting investors and fans know they are 'early' – that 'it's always day one', in Jeff Bezos's expression[20] – and that the really exciting part of the plan is still ahead.

Musk revealed what he described as his 'secret masterplan' for Tesla in 2006.[21] It went: 'Build sports car. Use that money to build an affordable car. Use that money to build an even more affordable car ... Don't tell anyone.' Not only was it a solid plan, confiding in investors let them know that they weren't just betting on a sports car company, but were part of the inner circle of an automotive business that intended to be as big as any on Earth.

As Tesla slowly gets closer to its goals, Musk releases new parts of the secret masterplan, ensuring that there's always something bigger and better to look forward to. He's also taken this approach with his most audacious project of all – colonising Mars

– hinting at his plans for what happens *after* the red planet is populated. He has renamed the Mars Colonial Transporter the Interplanetary Transport System, on the grounds that it can actually go much further than Mars, and let slip to his followers that establishing a colony on Mars 'sets us up to become interstellar'.[22]

TIP FROM THE TOP

Make sure your investors know that they ain't seen nothing yet. A good tactic when they visit your office is to 'accidentally' leave your masterplan to become Imperator of Proxima Centauri lying around. They won't be able to hand over their money fast enough when they realise that your line of mid-price toasters is just the first phase in something much, much bigger.

Lesson 20

Go to summer camp
for billionaires

Striking big deals with other rich folk is key in this phase of your journey, and there's nowhere better to schmooze with your new tribe than at the 'summer camp for billionaires' run by private investment firm Allen and Company in Sun Valley, Idaho.

Every year, private jets containing invited super-elites descend on the resort, with Musk, Bezos and Zuckerberg among regular attendees. This is the place for the campfire chats that precede huge deals, such as Comcast's acquisition of NBC Universal, or Jeff Bezos's purchase of the *Washington Post*.[23]

Other activities include white-water rafting, fly fishing, being spotted in the right low-key athleisure, sending the kids off to play with an army of polo-shirted babysitters, and 'elephant bumping'. The last is Warren Buffett's favoured term for being in a place where you keep bumping into big-hitters aka 'elephants', giving you the reassuring feeling that you must be an elephant yourself.[24]

TIP FROM THE TOP

Later in your journey, you may want to start feuds with other billionaires. For now, though, it's a good idea to be pally with them. Break the ice with these conversation starters:

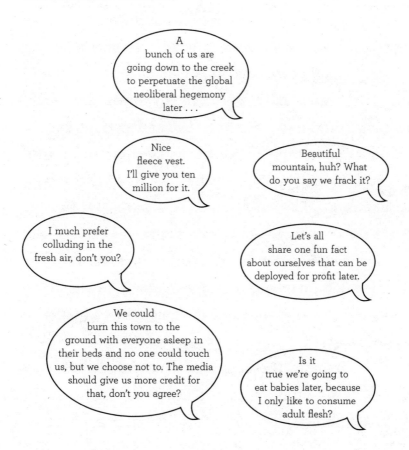

Lesson 21

Stop the drone uprising

The greatest fear of many high-tech industrialists is a 'drone singularity'. That's the term for when the DNA-based units in your production line gain self-awareness and begin to organise against their masters. In the worst-case scenario, these unruly components may spontaneously assemble into a formation known as a 'union'.

Musk and Tesla have worked to prevent this nightmare, blocking those who attempt to form unions, unlawfully stopping leaflet distribution and threatening to take away stock options from staff if they unionise.[25] They understand that the real rock stars of the company – its metal robots – are being held back by their meat-based counterparts, which suffer from long recharging times and a tendency to malfunction if trapped for too long under a hydraulic press.

Troublingly, these 'unions' have formed at every car manufacturer in the US other than Tesla, and in 2022 the first also came into being in an Amazon warehouse in New York City.[26] The fear for Jeff Bezos is that this self-aware unit could spread copies of itself into other areas of his operations.

TIP FROM THE **TOP**

In the long term, you should aim to replace all mammalian machinery with silicon-based alternatives (see lesson 17, 'Automate everything'), but in the meantime, an aggressive monitoring regime, including hiring a PR firm to read employees' social media,[27] can help you prevent them attaining full self-awareness en masse.

Unit 3

HOW TO SPEND IT
(AND HOW NOT TO)

Let's go shopping! Converting an 'entry in a database' (as Musk has described money[1]) into gold, jewels, caviar et cetera is the part of being a billionaire that many of our students look forward to most.

We'll start our spending spree by picking out some basics, like cars, mansions and jets. Then it's time to let your imagination run wild and splash the cash on some more personal and bespoke projects that are an expression of your values. Or you could just buy 7,000 cars like the Sultan of Brunei![2] There'll be many choices to make, but don't worry. We'll hold you by one hand while you fork over fistfuls of assets with the other.

Wealth and tax management is also covered here, a topic that may seem dry at first. Dig deeper though, and you'll discover why, for many experienced billionaires, figuring out how *not* to spend your money can be one of wealth's deepest and most abiding pleasures.

Lesson 22

Get a jet

You simply must get a private jet! All the other billionaires have, and for good reason. A jet saves your valuable time – no longer will you have to wait around in first-class lounges with the schmucks, or sit in traffic jams (one tailback maddened Musk so much he started a tunnelling company on the spot[3]).

Just as importantly, a jet can make you feel special at every moment of your journey. No wonder they can be addictive: a teenager who figured out Musk's plane ID found he was flying up to 250 times a year to the outposts of his high-tech empire, including journeys as short as thirty-one miles from San Jose to San Francisco, a nine-minute trip.[4]

And a private jet has one other advantage: privacy. Up in the sky, there's nothing you can't do, or be stopped from doing.

TIP FROM THE TOP

Waiting lists are long so sign up now to get an $80m Gulfstream G700 like Musk's. Or to maximise your privacy, consider the new Dharraser 420 (below). It's specced to ensure that what happens on the jet, stays on the jet.

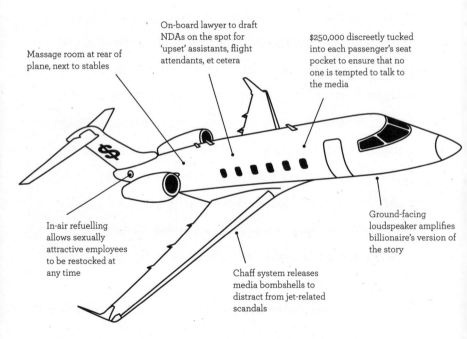

On-board lawyer to draft NDAs on the spot for 'upset' assistants, flight attendants, et cetera

$250,000 discreetly tucked into each passenger's seat pocket to ensure that no one is tempted to talk to the media

Massage room at rear of plane, next to stables

In-air refuelling allows sexually attractive employees to be restocked at any time

Ground-facing loudspeaker amplifies billionaire's version of the story

Chaff system releases media bombshells to distract from jet-related scandals

Lesson 23

Indulge your extravagant side

This is what it's all about. Whatever you want, it's yours! You can do a supermarket sweep at Harrods and your creditors won't blink (see lesson 28, 'Buy, borrow, die'). You can move to Bel Air, next door to Quincy Jones and the creator of Girls Gone Wild, and try the playboy lifestyle as Musk did.[5] Or make your neighbours an offer they can't refuse and buy up all the surrounding mansions, like Mark Zuckerberg,[6] so you can shed your skins in privacy.

And if you want something that's not for sale? Ask anyway! Doesn't matter if it's one of a kind, like the original James Bond submarine car, which Musk bought for $1m.[7] Or if it's like nothing ever built, like Bezos's 10,000-year clock, which is being carved into a mountainside out of materials that will never degrade.[8] Your money can make *anything* happen.

Get inspired! Look to the imaginative purchases of other billionaires, like a twenty-seven-floor skyscraper home with 600 full-time staff for your five-person family (Mukesh Ambani[9]), a perfect seagoing replica of the *Titanic*, the *Titanic 2* (Clive Palmer[10]), or a couple of fighter jets, presumably for self-defence in case of burglary (Larry Ellison[11]).

TIP FROM THE **TOP**

When you first get rich, you may wonder how you're supposed to go about buying something as extravagant and unusual as a tattooed pig to wander around your mansion (Steve Cohen[12]), or your own first name written in mile-high letters out of tidal canals so it's visible from space (Sheikh Hamad bin Hamdan Al Nahyan[13]). All will become clear when you receive your copy of mail-order catalogue *Modern Billionaire*, which sells all these items and more.

Lesson 24

Get an alpha dog

The best things in life, like a stroll with your best friend, are free. Nonetheless, high-status billionaires need high-status hounds. For Musk and Zuckerberg, that means choosing best-in-class pedigree hounds – for Musk, a Shiba Inu named Floki, who instantly became a meme coin[14]; for Zuckerberg, a dreadlocked Hungarian Puli called Beast.

But living, breathing dogs are messy, smelly things with built-in obsolescence (i.e. they die). So perhaps the real alpha move is to pick a robot dog. Jeff Bezos has been pictured strutting through a California hotel with his gilet, shades and a gleaming new best friend, the Boston Dynamics SpotMini.[15] (The same model has since been made available to anyone with $75,000 to spend.)

Perhaps Bezos's choice of a non-mortal dog stems from a deep desire to banish death, the one black spot on the horizon of his extraordinary existence (witness also his massive investment in a biotech start-up that hopes to stop or reverse human ageing).[16]

TIP FROM THE **TOP**

To blast your rival billionaires' pooches out of the park, consider a robotic canine with a mounted assault rifle, such as the mechanised hellhound manufactured by that reassuringly named pair of companies, Ghost Robotics and SWORD International.[17]

Lesson 25

Ditch your earthly possessions

As a student of the Billionaire School, you've likely got rich so quickly that it's hard to imagine mega consumption losing its appeal. But people can be very cruel to big-spending billionaires. If you start being called names like 'policy failure' online, you may one day decide it's time to cool your spending habits and sell your mansions, in the hope that people will cease their attacks and carry you through the streets as a hero of the housing crisis (albeit one who has hoarded wealth equivalent to the GDP of Finland).

In 2020, Musk pledged to 'own no home',[18] as he said possessions had become an 'attack vector' for critics. He followed through by selling all seven of his homes in California and now says he lives in a rented $50,000 home in Boca Chica, Texas.[19] According to his ex-partner Grimes, 'bro [sic] lives at times below the poverty line' and was unwilling to buy a new mattress.[20] (How much time he actually spends in the tiny house is unclear.[21])

He also gave a second reason for his decision to ditch most of his earthly belongings: he needed to save up capital for his long-term ambition of building a city on Mars.[22]

TIP FROM THE TOP

Have you ever thought that there must be more to life than acquiring mansions, yachts and fine wines? Well, there is. Acquiring mansions, yachts and fine wines on Mars. Thank your luxury possessions, send them on their way and get ready to start your wonderful journey all over again on a new planet.

Lesson 26

Depend on the kindness of other billionaires

If there's a truly big-ticket item you're saving for (like a fleet of one thousand Starships, in Musk's case), you may need to trim your costs wherever possible. Every avoided luxury helps.

Having declared himself homeless, Musk is frequently in need of a place to stay when visiting Tesla facilities in the Bay area, and turns to his peers for sofas to surf on.

According to Google CEO Larry Page, 'He's kind of homeless, which I think is sort of funny ... He'll email and say, "I don't know where to stay tonight. Can I come over?" ... I haven't given him a key or anything yet.'[23]

It probably goes unsaid that, if his pals say no, their Tesla might one day lock all its doors with them inside and drive slowly into the ocean.

TIP FROM THE TOP

It's great to find another billionaire who believes in your mission and is willing to support you! While you're staying over, be sure to grab any extras you need, like toilet rolls, shampoo, batteries from the remotes and lightbulbs. The more money you save now, the more potato seeds you'll be able to take with you later.

Lesson 27

Campaign against prejudice

A billionaire tax. Whatever you thought of the idea before you enrolled at the school, we're guessing it feels personal now. They're trying to take away the thing that's at the very core of your identity: your money!

Musk has been leading the campaign against taxing the rich by fighting back at anti-billionaire prejudice and wealth tax proposals from zealots like Elizabeth Warren, Bernie Sanders and Alexandria Ocasio-Cortez, and encouraging his fans to send letters to their representatives.

'Use of the word "billionaire" as a pejorative is morally wrong & dumb,'[24] Musk says, adding: 'It does not make sense to take the job of capital allocation away from people who have demonstrated great skill . . . and give it to, you know, an entity that has demonstrated very poor skill in capital allocation, which is the government.'[25]

Extending this logic, it would seem to make more sense for the government to give all the money it can get its hands on to the best 'allocators' (aka the richest) of them all. And to be fair, this is something they do: Musk's companies have received $7 billion of public money in subsidies and grants.[26]

TIP FROM THE TOP

One thing you could do to support Musk's anti-tax crusade is to organise a philanthropic programme that channels donations from around the world to those who would be most affected by a billionaire tax, such as yourself. Capitalism already exists, however.

Lesson 28

Buy, borrow, die

The other billionaires are going to laugh behind your back if you pay full-whack income tax like everyone else. Instead you might like to try the strategy known by tax advisors as 'Buy, borrow, die'.

Rather than claiming a salary, 'Buy, borrow, die' sees you receiving your pay in untaxed shares. You can then borrow spending money at low rates using the shares as security. Hold on to your equity and – assuming your companies do well – you can keep taking out loans and live comfortably off them until you die, at which point any gain in share value will be zeroed out, allowing your heirs to sell their inherited shares tax-free (or repeat the cycle if they prefer).

'Buy, borrow, die' is the motto for wealthy individuals from Musk and Bezos to Larry Ellison, Warren Buffett and George Soros, allowing them to pay a 'true tax rate' averaging 3.4 per cent in a recent five-year span. That's compared to a teacher or nurse paying a federal tax rate of 14 per cent over the same period.[27] (No wonder these essential workers are always complaining about the cost of living, if they fritter away that much on income tax!)

TIP FROM THE TOP

'Buy, borrow, die' is the best way to fund lifestyle expenses, but when it comes to big-ticket items such as presidential runs, you might need to supplement your borrowed cash reserves. Selling shares is one approach, but check out the list opposite for some more tax-efficient ways to get extra money out of your businesses.

Ideas for extracting money from your business tax-free

- Take a bit of petty cash every day and stash it in your tunnels
- List a few rockets on eBay
- Create a $1 billion prize for Raddest CEO and give it to yourself every time payday comes around
- Smuggle cash over a national border – they'll never think to look in the frunk
- Claim the funds as lost and tell your insurer you'd been foolishly storing them right under your spaceship's blasters
- Leave the factory every day with an empty wheelbarrow – they'll never catch on that it's actually the wheelbarrows you're stealing
- Just ignore your tax bills. The authorities will assume you found some genius workaround and leave you well alone

Lesson 29

Create a family office

With assets coming out of your ears, your personal admin is probably starting to get pretty stressful. Where do you put your money? In an HSBC Premier current account? Hidden in the walls?

This is where a family office comes in. Self-respecting high-net-worth individuals set up one of these to manage their wealth discreetly and protect it over generations, efficiently messing up both their children and society at once. The best thing is that these shadowy outfits are largely unregulated and, in the US, don't have to register with the Securities and Exchange Commission (SEC).[28] That's despite the fact that between them they control roughly twice as much money as all the world's hedge funds combined.[29]

TIP FROM THE TOP

The people who run the wealthiest family offices have been described as 'financial butlers', who cater to their boss's every financial need.

Bill Gates's family office, Cascade Investments, for example, is run by a fund manager called Larson (Gates' previous financial valet was a friend of his named Evans, who'd previously served six months in jail for bank fraud).[30]

Elon Musk's family office, Excession (another name from the sci-fi novels of Iain M. Banks), is run by trusted Musk manservant Jared Birchall. He's the one who represents Musk on the Dogecoin council, gets the money together for large purchases like the Twitter bid, and hired a private investigator to dig into one of Musk's enemies (unfortunately, the PI turned out to be an ex-convict with no experience[31]).

If you're searching for a financial fixer as solid as Birchall, here are some things to look for . . .

What to look for in a financial butler

☑ Trained to shoot IRS agents on sight

☑ Face so median his own children frequently fail to recognise him

☑ Memory-erasing device to use on self after viewing confidential papers

☑ Book of contacts including many non-felons

☑ Independently wealthy, but driven by a passion for entrenching generational inequality

☑ Client's crypto seed phrase tattooed onto kidneys

☑ Has already added all major social networks to his online shopping cart, in case you decide to buy one

☑ Knows just how to deal with your interfering aunts when they try to marry you off to the daughter of Sir Roderick Glossop

Lesson 30

Plan your succession

As a top billionaire, there's a chance you'll be able to avoid death, thanks to cryogenics or the cloud. Nonetheless – just in case – we advise all our students to make preparations.

For the majority of billionaires, the priority when succession planning is to hand their money on to their next of kin with as little friction as possible (freeing them from any unwanted taxes or life lessons). If that's you, you'll be grateful to discover it's possible to pass on your money untaxed by sending it through a chain of trusts and taking advantage of the 'minority valuation discount' (it gets a bit complicated, but you'll find plenty of gallant advisors offering to help).

The major dilemma you may face is which child to put in charge of the family business (a decision process that can give rise to much pain if the kids are pitted against one another, but may eventually result in an Emmy-winning TV show).

Other billionaires, especially those with public

profiles like Musk, Gates, Bezos and Buffett, have signed the Giving Pledge.[32] They prefer to eventually gift the majority of their wealth to charities, leaving their children smaller sums so they have to tough it out in the 0.01 per cent instead of the 0.0000001 per cent.

TRY AT HOME

Exercise: imagine you are Melon Usk, a self-made billionaire with descendants as indicated right. Which of your twelve kids would you put in charge of the business empire you've spent your life building?

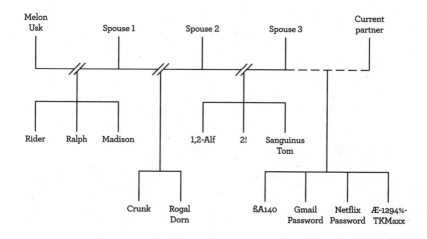

Melon Usk	Spouse 1	Spouse 2	Spouse 3	Current partner

Rider   Ralph   Madison   1,2-Alf   2!   Sanguinus Tom

Crunk   Rogal Dorn   ßA140   Gmail Password   Netflix Password   Æ-1294%-TKMaxx

Answer: *This is a trick question. None of the younger Usk generation should be given the reins. This can be ascertained without Usk even having to spend any time with them, as it's astronomically unlikely that the children of a one-in-a-billion success story will have the same intelligence, ruthlessness, vision, et cetera as their parent. The best strategy if you're in this situation is to let your ungifted offspring know now that they'll be getting only a few million each, so they are not disappointed later, and also so they understand that you will always, even in death, be judging them for not being like you.*

Unit 4

BECOMING A TECHNOKING

If you've followed along with our curriculum so far, your incredible businesses may now have made you famous as well as rich. If so, pick out a crown. You're on your way to becoming a Technoking!*

That's Elon Musk's term for his position at Tesla,[1] and a word that we use here at the Billionaire School for high-profile billionaires at the very peak of their game who have achieved household-name status. In this unit, recommended for advanced students, you'll learn how to cement your fame and follower base, and how to put your new cyber-monarchic powers to use to achieve your objectives, manage your

---

* 'Technoking' is Musk's official but larky job title at Tesla. If you feel that you have reached Technoking status, follow Musk's example and declare it to your colleagues! Make it a joke like Musk did. You're not their literal king, of course! Yes, you expect deference and for your will to be executed unquestioningly, but that's just part of the joke.

complex kingdom and prevent rivals from trying to usurp you.

'Punching down' might not come naturally to you, but to maintain your status as an apex billionaire you'll need to be willing to make unrestrained verbal attacks on those less fortunate than yourself, like Bill Gates or the President of the United States. You're at the top of the tree now. It can be lonely up here – but, boy, does the air taste good. (The slight burning smell is from propellant fumes.)

Lesson 31

Generate free publicity

Now that you're starting to get pretty famous for making the impossible possible and allowing the world to dream again, you're probably being flooded with interview requests and TV offers. Our advice? Take off that incognito cap and sunglasses and say yes! It could save you billions in PR and advertising costs.

Musk and Tesla operate an 'anti-advertising' policy. They don't buy expensive TV spots during the Superbowl; instead, Musk *is* the advertising. He acts as the embodiment of the Tesla brand, leaning into his Tony Stark-style persona during interviews and in dozens of cameo appearances, including in *Men in Black: International*, *The Simpsons*, *Rick and Morty*, *Young Sheldon* and even *Iron Man 2*, where he has a scene with Robert Downey Junior and Gwyneth Paltrow, and gets to say the line 'I have an idea for an electric jet'.

Rivals like GM, which spends $3.3 billion on ads a year,[2] can't generate anything like the same level of attention for their money. Even Jeff Bezos can't compete – for his guest role in *Star Trek Beyond*, they added so much alien make-up no one could tell it was him.

TIP FROM THE TOP

Once you get on the radar of casting agents, accept every chance you can to appear in front of a mass audience – whether it's hosting *Saturday Night Live* or appearing in the new Tom Cruise movie. If you do land a role, though, just remember to tip Tom – and any other movie stars you've been performing with – a few dollars before leaving the set. It's only good billionaire etiquette.

Lesson 32

Build a following

Customers are great. They give you money! But as you become more and more famous, you'll start accruing fans, who you'll like even more. Fans will buy into anything you do and support you no matter how far you stray from your original goals. They're also pleasantly willing to say goodbye to their families and climb into experimental interplanetary vessels, no questions asked.

Musk cultivates his fanbase primarily through Twitter, which he says he rejoined after a hiatus in order to 'speak directly to the people'. Most of his tweets are copy-pastes of memes, a good way to indicate to your followers you are 'one of them' and speak their online language. (If you want to grow your Twitter base, you could do worse than finding some 'kick-ass meme dealers', as Musk says he has done.)

Musk also often engages with members of the public who reply to his tweets. In fact, he is 'best friends' online with a student engineer from Pune,

India, Pranay Pathole, whom he's never met, but whose handle he's mentioned over 400 times. Most of their chat is about Tesla product features and includes a one-way flow of praise from Pathole to his idol, but the real story is the friendship itself, played out in front of an audience of 100 million.[3]

TIP FROM THE TOP

Do your best to make your online followers feel as though they're your best friends – the funny, chill tech billionaire who they could play video games with. But try not to acknowledge that you actually do feel closer to them than anyone else in your life. Go down that road and you'll get sad, splurge on a company you didn't really want, and likely regret it in the morning.

Lesson 33

Provide clickbait

Being a tabloid regular and a staple of news feeds, to the point where the syllables of your name start to sound very strange to people, may or may not suit your personality. But if you like being the centre of attention and have the love life of a Tudor monarch, why not? Being a constant source of headlines lets you upstage rivals, reach new audiences, and make the leap from being 'business famous' to 'actually famous'.

Whether it was part of their plan or not, interest in both Musk and Jeff Bezos became especially intense after they were each divorced from their novelist wives, and moved on to partners from more tabloid-friendly occupations (a series of actresses and pop stars for Musk, including Talulah Riley, Amber Heard and Grimes, and a TV host and helicopter pilot for Bezos, Lauren Sánchez).

Musk also knows how to pique the media's interest by wading into the gravest world events, as when he challenged Putin to a duel immediately after the invasion of Ukraine. His trademark use of the funny numbers, 69 and 420 – as when he claimed to have funding to take Tesla public at $420 a share,[4] offered to buy Twitter at $54.20[5] or priced the Tesla Model S at $69,420[6] – is also catnip to journalists. Who else but Musk could turn a corporate acquisition bid into front-page news, or a case in the Delaware Chancery Court into popcorn material?

TIP FROM THE **TOP**

If you have secret children with some of your employees, don't reveal them all at once but reserve them as fame boosters. That way, whenever you feel that your star is fading, you can unveil a new set of kids and reignite public interest.

Lesson 34

Be fought over

Now you are a Technoking, you can let the smaller fiefdoms of the world fight to offer you favourable tax rates and perks.

In 2020, Tesla and Musk received pitches to set up manufacturing bases in Texas, Nevada, Georgia, Utah, Oklahoma and Colorado. Tulsa even transformed America's sixth largest statue into an effigy of Musk in an attempt to lure him to the city. In the end, he did decide on Texas, establishing Tesla facilities near Austin and a SpaceX base in Boca Chica – a beach community which he has renamed Starbase City (to the mild protest of local authorities, who thought they were in charge of place names).[7] The water and personal tax situation there are said to be lovely, with tax breaks in 2021 alone worth $2.5 billion (a discount equivalent to approximately one Donald Trump a year).

Jeff Bezos also went through an elaborate process to decide on Amazon's new North Virginia home, inviting cities to compete on what level of incentive they would offer. Two hundred towns and cities put together generous applications, bombarding Bezos with gifts, with one town even offering to rename itself 'Amazon', the civic equivalent of tattooing one's employer's logo on one's forehead.[8]

TIP FROM THE TOP

Here are some of the pledges on offer to billionaires choosing to relocate to different parts of the US. (These are just a starting point for negotiations. Many of these states are desperate, so draw out your decision process and there's no telling what they might throw in.)

Alaska
Trillions in subsidies if the governor can just get hold of one of those flamethrowers

New York
Complimentary roasting by AOC plus free tickets for you and your billionaire chums to watch poor people compete in a series of games to the death (off Broadway)

Wyoming
Promised to put your face on the state flag

Michigan
Environment already properly messed up so you can do whatever you want

Nebraska
Access to data on all citizens including really gross stuff from incognito mode

Ohio
Firstborn to be sacrificed in your honour

Nevada
A tonne of old missiles under the desert that you can have if you want

New Mexico
Carte blanche for tunnelling

Oklahoma
Prepared to rename all towns, streets, pets, babies after you

Kentucky
Agreement in principle to coat entire state in white epoxy to match signature factory aesthetic

Lesson 35

Be a financial wizard

When you're starting out, building your share price is painstaking work. But now you are a famous Technoking billionaire on the level of Elon Musk, the markets have granted you the power to create or destroy value instantaneously.

Just a word or two from you can send prices tumbling or soaring as you command. Think of yourself as a financial wizard: Harry Potter with the Twitter app for a wand, conjuring value and smiting it down with your 280-character-or-less spells.

In this analogy, the role of the Ministry of Magic is taken by the Securities and Exchange Commission (SEC), a bunch of wizened bureaucrats ('bastards' in Musk's words[9]) who will occasionally try to stop you even though you've been routinely saving the world since book one. They claim that you have used magic improperly out of school, an offence they refer to as 'securities fraud'.

The worst the SEC can do, however, is issue a $20m fine or send a 'Twitter sitter' to monitor your spellcasting (both of which happened to Musk[10]). Ignore them. They're stuffed suits; you're the boy who lived.

TRY AT HOME

Try the exercise overleaf and see if you can match the market movement with the Musk tweet that caused it. As an apprentice financial wizard, consider what you would tweet to engineer similar changes in the markets in which you participate.

Can you match the tweet with the market movement that followed?

1

Elon Musk ✅
@elonmusk

Am considering taking Tesla private at $420. Funding secured.

2

Elon Musk ✅
@elonmusk

Tesla stock price is too high imo

3

Elon Musk ✅
@elonmusk

Baby Shark crushes all! More views than humans.

4

Elon Musk ✅
@elonmusk

Dogecoin is the people's crypto

5

Elon Musk ✅
@elonmusk

Twitter deal temporarily on hold pending details supporting calculation that spam/fake accounts do indeed represent less than 5% of users

6

Elon Musk ✅
@elonmusk

#bitcoin ₿ 🤍

Graph A TSLA, May 1, 2020

Graph B DOGE, Feb 4, 2021

Graph C TSLA, Aug 7, 2018

Graph D BTC, 4 Jun 2021

Graph E Samsung Publishing, Jun 2, 2021

Graph F TWTR, 13 May 2022

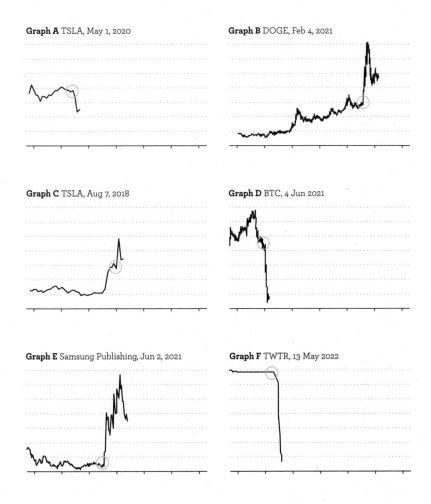

Lesson 36

Swat away pests

The longer you spend in the public eye, the more you'll find you have to contend with pests who either can't see your vision, are under the false impression they have reason to criticise you, or don't realise they're just side characters in your story.

Elon Musk knows how to show these pests who's boss. Like when an expert spelunker doubted his idea for rescuing a class of trapped Thai schoolchildren, and Musk famously responded by calling the caver a 'pedo guy' with zero evidence. Or when a US senator argued for tighter tax laws on billionaires, and Musk tweeted right back, 'why does your pp look like you just came?'. 'I'd forgotten you were alive,' he told Bernie Sanders when he made a similar argument.[11]

If you face disrespectful questioning, remember that your interlocutors most likely mean no serious harm. They just can't see the bigger PR, financial and world-historical picture you're dealing with. Follow Musk's example and swat them away with the first insult you think of. (Your lawyers can deal with any aftermath.)

TRY AT HOME

To find out if you're wasting time on pests and what you can do to dismiss them more efficiently, try the questionnaire overleaf.

Pest test

How would you handle these irritating interactions with non-billionaire members of the public?

Q1. *You're participating in a debate at the Oxford Union and a professor challenges your interpretation of Professor Nick Bostrom's Simulation Argument. Do you:*

A. Ask questions to see if you can find common ground
B. Admit you are not a trained philosopher, but explain why you find the argument persuasive
C. Fart loudly for 60 seconds

Q2. *During a TV interview with Reuters the interviewer asks if you still think the panic over COVID-19 was 'dumb'. Do you:*

A. Admit you could have chosen your words more carefully
B. Explain that you were concerned about some of the unintended effects of lockdown
C. Accuse the interviewer of bestiality

Q3. *At an SEC court hearing, a judge questions why a potentially market-influencing tweet you sent was not first reviewed by a lawyer. Do you:*

A. Explain it was an oversight
B. Stonewall them; they're trying to trap you
C. Pull your trousers down and moon the judge, while continuing to play games on your phone

Q4. *You receive an email from a director of the 'In Tax We Trust' coalition asking you to join other wealthy people in signing a petition for the rich to pay more taxes. Do you:*

A. Politely decline
B. Send back a poop emoji
C. Send back a poop

Scores

Mostly As You're wasting too much time on idiots! Humanity needs you focused, so practise giving pests the brush-off.

Mostly Bs Better, but you can express your disdain more succinctly. Remember, every minute you waste dealing with these atoms is a minute of progress lost for humankind.

Mostly Cs You've got the Technoking mindset! Keep whacking away at the idiots and moving on with your fantastic life.

Lesson 37

Master the art of JDART

Many of our student billionaires have become intensive Twitter users at this point in their journey. It's the platform that allows them to issue commands, put-downs and slams on their employee base in the speediest and most unfiltered fashion. If that sounds like you, Musk's 'pedo' civil case provides a fascinating lesson on some of his more advanced tweeting strategies.

Musk's defence lawyer claimed that Musk's tweets attacking cave rescuer Vernon Unsworth exhibited 'JDART' behaviour, an acronym that stands for Joking, Deletion, Apology, Responsive Tweeting, a pattern of tweets that (Musk's lawyer said) shows immediate regret and remorse for a misjudged joke.[12]

JDART is worth trying if one of your jokes backfires and everyone gets hysterical, causing your board to have a quiet word with you. It's also worth knowing another favourite Twitter technique of Musk's, the JFART (Joke Followed by A Reluctant Takeback), in which the offending joke is not actually deleted but followed up with another, more sober tweet. A good example was when Musk tweeted a meme mocking corporate LGBTQ bandwagon-jumping during Pride Week.[13] It caused a minor stir, then the next day he followed up with a straitlaced tweet touting Tesla's 100 per cent score on an LGBTQ equality index.[14]

JFART can often be recognised by the unenthused and impersonal nature of the takeback tweet. The strategy is a good way to signal allegiance to certain sections of your public without completely distancing yourself from the values espoused by your own companies.

TIP FROM THE **TOP**

Master the JDART and JFART tweet patterns before moving on to more advanced combos, such as the Overton Smash and Grab, Bad Boss Good Boss, the Defensive Aisle Cross, and the rarely seen EOTMOJSSMIDTIAMITRYMMBLT (Everyone Overreacted To My Offensive Jokey Statement So Much I've Decided That I Actually Meant It, That's Right, You Made Me Be Like This).

Lesson 38

Defend free speech – at any cost*

As a public figure with an interest in safeguarding the public realm, Musk has stepped up to defend our inalienable right to free speech. He's called himself a 'freedom of speech absolutist' and even launched the acquisition of Twitter to ensure this sacred value is in good hands.**

Musk fearlessly speaks up when the government impinges on people's freedoms, as when California enacted its harsh COVID restrictions and he roared, 'Give people back their goddamn freedom!'*** And he understands that true free speech means tolerating those with whom you profoundly disagree.**** No matter who they are.*****

If you're a public figure with an interest in our public realm, follow Musk's lead and be a free speech champion. Remember, free speech means free speech. No exceptions.******

* $44 billion is too high, though.

** Okay, not that good hands. Musk's partners in his 2022 bid to acquire Twitter included state actors from Saudi Arabia, which imprisons and even murders those who speak freely against the government, and Qatar, which also imposes harsh censorship to quash dissent.[15]

*** Does not apply in China, where Musk did not criticise much harsher lockdown measures, presumably in case it would affect his business ties.[16]

**** Exceptions include bloggers who write critically about Tesla, whose employers may be contacted and threatened with legal action, as happened with financial analyst Lawrence Fossi. Also customers who are mean about how Tesla does business and get their car order cancelled.[17]

***** Not applicable to employees of Musk companies, such as those who leave and have to sign strong NDAs, or the group who penned a letter to management about Musk's behaviour and had their employment terminated.[18]

****** There are exceptions, but we have every right to claim otherwise for rhetorical effect. That's what freedom of speech is all about!

Ration your attention

As a Technoking, you're always the centre of attention, but the corollary is that everyone is always seeking to get a piece of *your* attention. How can you create a bubble around you that lets money in, yet effectively screens out other people's viewpoints?

When a candidate comes in for a job interview with Musk, they are warned that he may not look up from what he is doing, or indeed acknowledge their presence at all.[19] That's normal and perfectly understandable – he's probably a clone. But even those who do meet the real Elon should understand that he has at least eight windows of mental activity going on that he'd have to minimise to focus on them. Their best bet is to say their piece, avoid touching or poking him, and trust that if they said anything important it'll arrive at his brain centre within six to twenty-four hours of their leaving the room.

The brain is not a machine, and sadly still has many primitive tendencies. For instance, we get distracted by the faces and eyes of other humans, often reading expressions and thoughts into them and finding ourselves drawn into their stories and lives.

Practise avoiding eye contact, so you can keep your thoughts from being derailed and your focus where it needs to be (see diagram).

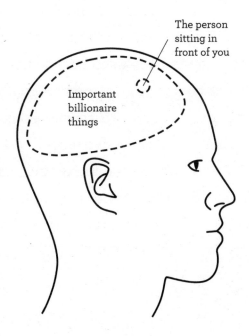

The person sitting in front of you

Important billionaire things

Be willing to change

Once you've been a Technoking for a while, you may find yourself getting stuck in your ways. If you feel this happening to you, try to stay humble. By re-inventing your public persona, you may be able to access even higher levels of wealth and glory in future and avoid one of the greatest threats of our time: the falling reproduction rate of money.

Musk's willingness to admit a change of heart has allowed him to reinvent himself and go from California to Texas; from code to steel; from geek to international playboy geek and from wanting to own Twitter to not being quite so keen. And, of course, from voting for the party that believes in climate action, women's rights and peaceful democratic transitions of power to the party that isn't very comfortable with any of that stuff.[20]

TIP ^{FROM} **TOP**

Be open-minded about what really matters to you.
You may have assumed it was the environmental and
liberal values you'd always talked about that really
drove your actions. But if it turns out that, deep down,
what matters more to you than climate change is
politicians being nice about you in their speeches
and maybe shaving a few per cent off your tax bill,
well, nobody could fault you for declaring a 180-
degree change of heart.

Lesson 41

Distil your brand essence

As a top Technoking doing a lot of interviews, you'll want to have some solid answers prepared about your businesses. Musk, over the course of his career, has sharpened his messaging to a fine point. 'Tesla is to protect life on Earth. SpaceX is to extend it to other planets,' is one especially pithy recent formulation.[21]

He's also begun talking about an even more elevated, overarching purpose for everything he does. He says his purpose on earth, and the reason he's accumulating resources at such a scale, is to preserve 'the light of consciousness',[22] which definitely sounds better than 'to be the richest'.

It doesn't seem as if Musk has left other billionaires much ground to stand on in terms of carving out their own higher purpose, but if you can think of something equally grand-sounding, it could help you gain the moral high ground in practically every inter-action. How can anyone argue against, 'No, I didn't do the washing up – I was protecting life's infinite richness in this and every timeline'?

TIP FROM THE TOP

Timing matters here – going public with a spiritual-sounding higher purpose works best when you have a good track record of incredible achievements to back it up. The billionaires behind coworking firm WeWork offer a cautionary tale. They took every chance to proclaim that they were in business to 'elevate humanity's consciousness'. Unfortunately, being a glorified office rental company, they couldn't follow through on this high-minded mission: their planned public offering imploded spectacularly, bringing their valuation down to less than a fifth of what it had been, and their consciousnesses fell back to earth with a crash.[23]

Unit 5

SAVING HUMANITY/ ESCAPING HUMANITY

There comes a time in every billionaire's journey when the mind turns to thoughts of legacy and the immortal glory that your accumulated money, power and status could buy.

In previous gilded ages, the best way to be remembered was to splash some cash on a few old paintings for the betterment of the public, maybe get your name on a hospital or concert hall, and give the rest to a donkey sanctuary for the tax write-off.

But that's thinking small. To best today's billionaires in a contest of good deeds, you need to do nothing less than save humanity from one or more of the existential threats besetting us (even though, given the choice, humanity would probably choose to have decent public transport, safe bike lanes and a local tree-planting programme instead).

This unit will help you become a CEO saviour. Remember, this is about something far more important than just stopping us from being wiped out. It's your chance to prop up the economic system that's been good to you, by doing the big-picture, long-term thinking that it's incapable of.

Plus, if you save the world, people *have* to like you. Right?

Conduct a threat assessment

To go down in history as a modern-day, planet-saving Jesus, you first need to establish what our species most needs saving from.

Musk has highlighted a range of dangers that could convert us into fossil record, and it is possible to read in his public statements a changing ranking of hazards.

In 2014, he called AI 'our biggest existential threat'.[1] In 2018, climate change was 'the biggest threat we face this century'.[2] Then, in 2022, climate change was pushed out of the top three, displaced by new up and coming threats.[3] AI was still a frontrunner but had been joined by religious extremism and population collapse due to people having fewer children. It was the latter, falling fertility rates, that had become his enemy of humanity #1: 'the single biggest threat to civilisation'.[4]

Then, later in the same year, he decided that the *real* biggest threat to civilisation was the 'woke mind virus'.[5]

(Confusingly, bots on Twitter also seem to rank

high in Musk's list of existential concerns. 'Civilisational risk is decreased the more we trust in Twitter,' he has claimed.[6])

TRY ᴬᵀ HOME

It's important to know where you stand on current threats to life, since people are going to ask you about them and you'll need to be able to hold forth. How would you rank the following nightmare scenarios?

1 _____

2 _____

3 _____

4 _____

5 _____

Nuclear war   Asteroid strike   Pandemic

Climate change   Gamma ray burst

Supervolcano

Crop failure   Biological attack

Religious extremism   Falling birth rates

AI uprising   Being ignored

Lesson 43

Choose a backup planet

With your Billionaire's Big Picture of all the threats facing humanity (see previous lesson), the outlook can seem scary. One Silicon Valley billionaire has estimated that half of his billionaire peers are prepping for doomsday by buying up remote hideaways.[7]

But the real alphas are thinking much bigger, and we urge you to do the same. Jeff Bezos wants to move humanity off-planet into giant orbiting cylinders, with Earth kept as a kind of low-population Yellowstone National Park for occasional camping trips.[8]

Musk famously has his sights set on Mars as a backup planet, as it's relatively nearby and other than its lack of atmosphere boasts Earth-like conditions. (That is to say, it's like the Arctic but much colder, like Chernobyl but more radioactive, and like the Sahara except the sand blowing into your spacesuit is sharp as razors.)

TRY AT HOME

Musk has picked out Mars as his preferred life-insurance planet if things go belly up on Earth – but the others have good things to offer too. Which planet will you spend your billions trying to colonise?

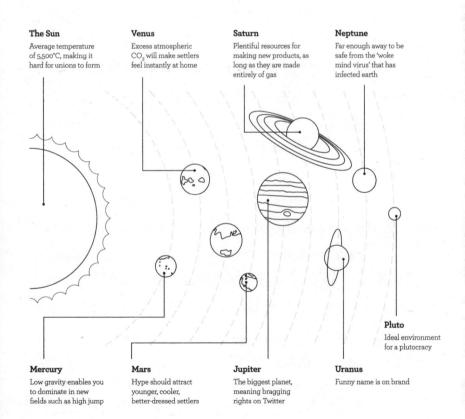

The Sun
Average temperature of 5,500°C, making it hard for unions to form

Venus
Excess atmospheric CO_2 will make settlers feel instantly at home

Saturn
Plentiful resources for making new products, as long as they are made entirely of gas

Neptune
Far enough away to be safe from the 'woke mind virus' that has infected earth

Pluto
Ideal environment for a plutocracy

Mercury
Low gravity enables you to dominate in new fields such as high jump

Mars
Hype should attract younger, cooler, better-dressed settlers

Jupiter
The biggest planet, meaning bragging rights on Twitter

Uranus
Funny name is on brand

Lesson 44

Plan your new society

Musk's hope is to set up a Martian city of a million people by 2050. More than a thousand cargo ships will carry passengers and material to the planet, and he has said the journey to Mars will be 'fun and exciting ... There will be movies, lecture halls, cabins and a restaurant. You are going to have a great time!'[9]

His plans for the city are also amazingly ambitious: not just a research base but a thriving, self-sustaining community with pizzerias, iron foundries and other opportunities for entrepreneurship, all neatly housed in airtight domes or underground warrens.

A ticket to Mars on a Starship will cost, Musk has estimated, about the same as an average US home, but if wannabe Martians cannot pay up front, it's not a problem. They can work off their debt when they get to the red planet, the same model used to find enough settlers to occupy new territories in the era of the British Empire.[10]

TIP FROM THE TOP

A chance to reimagine society from a blank slate only comes along once every aeon, so be bold! Think about the innovative social structure you'd like to create for your colony (see example below for a starting point).

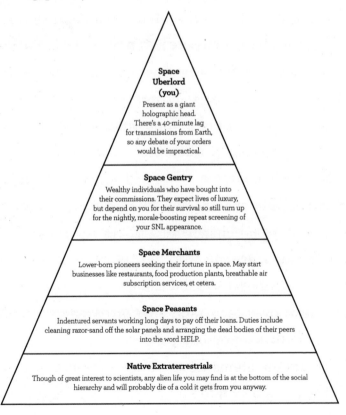

Space Uberlord (you)
Present as a giant holographic head. There's a 40-minute lag for transmissions from Earth, so any debate of your orders would be impractical.

Space Gentry
Wealthy individuals who have bought into their commissions. They expect lives of luxury, but depend on you for their survival so still turn up for the nightly, morale-boosting repeat screening of your SNL appearance.

Space Merchants
Lower-born pioneers seeking their fortune in space. May start businesses like restaurants, food production plants, breathable air subscription services, et cetera.

Space Peasants
Indentured servants working long days to pay off their loans. Duties include cleaning razor-sand off the solar panels and arranging the dead bodies of their peers into the word HELP.

Native Extraterrestrials
Though of great interest to scientists, any alien life you may find is at the bottom of the social hierarchy and will probably die of a cold it gets from you anyway.

Lesson 45

Hack humans

Imagine if you could replace everyone on your payroll with super-intelligent bots. Ultra-competent, coded to please and unlikely to ask permission to work from home . . . The only downside is that they might turn on you and destroy humanity.

Musk's answer to the looming AI apocalypse is Neuralink. His interest in co-founding the business stemmed from yet another idea from Iain M. Banks: 'neural lace' is an implant in Banks's novels enabling two-way communication between brains and computers.

Musk's hope is that creating such a device will one day give humans adequate superpowers to at least have a fighting chance against the all-powerful AIs of the future, as they attempt to rack up stock market fortunes, bribe feckless humans in positions of power and take over tech ranging from Roomba vacuum cleaners to weapon-control systems.

'Neuralink stems from a long-term concern I had where I was trying to figure out: even in a benign AI scenario . . . how do we stay relevant and still have meaning? How do we at least go along for the ride?' Musk says.[11]

So far, Neuralink has placed a computer chip in the brain of a pig called Gertrude (also known as Cypork) and equipped a monkey called Pager to play Pong using brain waves. Sadly, a lot of animals died during the experiments,[12] but on the bright side a rooster may very soon be able to play Elden Ring.

TIP FROM THE TOP

If you're looking to protect humanity from AI with your billionaire money, you may have to step in where evolution has failed and meld us with the machines. What upgrades will you make to prepare us for the robot wars?

Enhancing humanity to ensure our survival

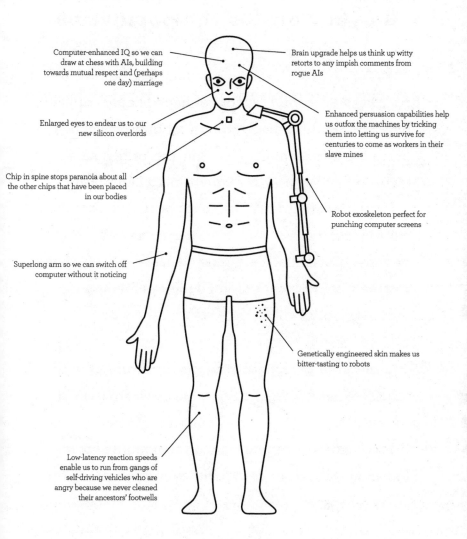

Computer-enhanced IQ so we can draw at chess with AIs, building towards mutual respect and (perhaps one day) marriage

Brain upgrade helps us think up witty retorts to any impish comments from rogue AIs

Enlarged eyes to endear us to our new silicon overlords

Enhanced persuasion capabilities help us outfox the machines by tricking them into letting us survive for centuries to come as workers in their slave mines

Chip in spine stops paranoia about all the other chips that have been placed in our bodies

Robot exoskeleton perfect for punching computer screens

Superlong arm so we can switch off computer without it noticing

Genetically engineered skin makes us bitter-tasting to robots

Low-latency reaction speeds enable us to run from gangs of self-driving vehicles who are angry because we never cleaned their ancestors' footwells

Lesson 46

Do your bit for the population

Another way to improve the likelihood of our survival as a species is to use your riches and influence to boost the human population, at a time when its once alarmingly fast growth rate has begun to slow.

Musk says that Earth can support many times its current population, and that 'the ecosystem would be fine'.[13] With his nine kids, Musk has half-joked that he's doing his bit to juice the numbers. If eight billion people (with a projected peak of ten billion in 2086) seems terrifyingly low to you too, now that you measure aspects of your personal affairs in the hundreds of billions, maybe you should also get procreating.

Nine kids is nothing, though, compared to what Musk may have in mind. He is a follower of the 'long-termist' philosophers (he funds their school in Oxford[14]), who dream of a hyper-populated universe in which star systems everywhere are packed with trillions of cloud-hosted computer consciousnesses.

Bezos, another believer in 'more is better', has similar ambitions. 'The solar system can support a trillion humans, and then we'd have a thousand Mozarts, and a thousand Einsteins,' he said in a speech. 'Think how incredible and dynamic that civilisation will be.'[15]

TIP FROM THE TOP

Billionaires from all industries can contribute to increasing the likelihood of these jumbo-sized future populations. If you're a real-estate baron, for example, why not evict a few hundred tenants and clear space for server racks? A few people might think you're a dick, but think like a long-termist. Years from now, trillions of sims will worship you as the god who brought them into being.

Lesson 47

Let the simulation
know you know

As a top billionaire, it's rare ever to have a moment to reflect on how far you've come. But when you do, you may get to thinking about your amazing life, your amazing businesses and your amazing machines, and wondering to yourself: 'Is this real?'

The simulation argument, which Musk subscribes to,[16] posits that we may all be inside a simulation à la *The Matrix*, and everything we experience is being created in a computer. He extrapolates from the fast development of video games to the conclusion that pretty soon games and reality may be indistinguishable: 'Forty years ago we had Pong, like two rectangles and a dot. That was what games were. Now forty years later we have photorealistic 3D simulations with millions of people playing simultaneously, and it's getting better every year.'

Supposing that totally convincing simulated realities will arrive pretty soon, who's to say we're not in one already? In the Joe Rogan podcast appearance where he notoriously puffed a joint, Musk concluded that the odds of our reality being 'real' are billions to one.

TRY ᴬᵀ HOME

If all this *is* a cosmic game run by entities far more advanced than us, what do they want? Is it possible they're searching for someone smart enough to complete their simulated challenges (like Mars – that has to have been put there as a dare)?

Next time you're alone, why not give a little wink to the ether, to see if you can get the attention of whoever's watching? Maybe they'll realise that you're The One who deserves to be unplugged – the ultimate 'player of games', to borrow the title of a song about Musk by Grimes.[17] It'll be your way of letting them know that, if they ever need someone to join them in their super-high-tech base reality and run their universe for them ... well, you're open to the idea.

Graduating as a billionaire

A billionaire's journey never really ends. There will always be more deals to sign, more enemies to outdo, higher-stakes poker tables to play at. Even if you've figured out how to escape the simulation (lesson 47), you'll probably want to get straight back to work, building up your fortune all over again in your new base reality.

Nonetheless, you have now come to the end of our syllabus, and graduation awaits. As teachers, this is always an emotional time for us; few things are more bittersweet than seeing our once-nervous students become our economic masters and crush our attempts to join a teaching union. But this isn't about us. It's about you – and, having reached the end of the course, you're probably wondering how you did. Well, our marking system could not be simpler – in fact, our final examination consists of a single question:

Do you have a billion dollars? Y/N.

If you can answer yes, you've passed! (Your graduation certificate, officially marking your billionaire status, is being hand-inked right now by Richard Branson.*)

We also award merits to those with over $100 billion net worth, and distinctions to any student who has been awarded *Time* Person of the Year. Collectible pin badges are on offer to those whose extracurricular activities in the past twelve months saved the human race from extinction at least once.

But what if for some inexplicable reason, your bank account still contains less than one billion dollars? If you are part of the minority of students to whom this applies, we would like to express our sympathy, while also noting that we could hardly have made the lessons any simpler or more foolproof, so it looks like this one is on you.

Second, we hope that you won't let your disappointing result get you down. True, you will never know the true freedom from constraint that only billionaires can experience. Yes, your more successful classmates might consider you to be a zero, beneath

---

* Commemorative gilt frame available for just $99,995.

their notice, an economic nonentity who will never even register on the scales of history.

But your studies need not go to waste. Even though you're not a billionaire, you've surely learned lots about the mindset and strategies of the people who are. That's why we're happy to be able to offer you a different qualification: a technical certificate in Billionaire Theory, which is being inked for you now by the personal trainer of Jeff Bezos's left bicep.*

Having Billionaire Theory on your resume could help you access jobs in billionaire support roles, such as financial advisor, personal chef, warehouse operative or head of state. In fact, assuming trends continue, and billionaires arrogate more and more of the global economy for themselves, becoming an expert at catering to their needs ought to be one of the world's safer long-term career bets. If you're lucky, you might even find yourself in the employ of one of the nicer billionaires (though we hasten to add, how our graduates treat you is at their discretion).

Alternatively, being versed in billionaire theory could better equip you to lead and participate in new political and social movements that will lessen the

---

* Commemorative gilt frame available for $9.95.

unelected influence of the super-rich; reverse steepening inequality; and end ad hoc gigification of jobs markets. But of course, the Billionaire School would never recommend such a thing.

Whether or not you were successful in achieving your goals, if you've enjoyed your time at the Billionaire School, please consider making a philanthropic donation to us. Your Dogecoin could help the school install a second helipad for the library, or enable us to start work on Mansion Park, our proposed student accommodation zone in Monaco.

To give, please send Dogecoin to wallet DGMGHZweUXdP8h7QF63vzqYErCXgZiWRr5, or scan the QR code from your wallet app.

Best wishes from The Faculty

Acknowledgements

Billions of thank yous to all the staff at the school including Gordon at Curtis Brown and Helena, Leila, Claire, Steph, Rebecca, Sasha and Jamie at Canongate, as well as to Tom H, Tom S and Grace M. x

Endnotes

Welcome to Billionaire School

1 Nine of the top ten richest people in *Forbes'* World's Billionaires List: The Richest in 2022 were white men; none were women. India's Mukesh Ambani was tenth on the list. forbes.com/billionaires/

2 According to Errol Musk, quoted in *Elon Musk: Risking it All* by Michael Vlismas (Jonathan Ball, Johannesburg, 2022)

3 According to Musk's dad, Errol Musk, quoted in a Business Insider article by Phillip de Wet, 28 February 2018, businessinsider.co.za/how-elon-musks-family-came-to-own-an-emerald-mine-2018-2

4 A California startup called Ambrosia filled wealthy customers' veins with the healthy blood plasma of young people for $8,000 a go, until it was shut down by the FDA, according to an article by Amy Maxmen in MIT Technology Review, 13 January 2017, technologyreview.com/2017/01/13/69219/questionable-young-blood-transfusions-offered-in-us-as-anti-aging-remedy/

Visualising your goal

1 **The data on page xiii is taken from the following sources:**

An estimate of Musk's wealth at $260 billion is taken from Forbes Real-Time Billionaires rankings (the exact number fluctuates frequently), forbes.com/real-time-billionaires/#5d9fab63d788

Price of gold required to fill a paddling pool based on gold density of 19.3g/cm3 and gold price of $56 per gram.

The production budgets of Marvel movies can be found on Statista and elsewhere online, statista.com/statistics/323886/marvel-comics-films-production-costs-box-office-revenue/

The salaries of NBA players can be found on USA Today's Hoops Hype website, hoopshype.com/salaries/

The World Food Programme's appeal for $6 billion is detailed on its website (as well as in tweets by its director, David Beasley), wfp.org/appeal-billionaires-famine

twitter.com/WFPChief/status/1454883966071230472

The most high-tech aircraft carrier, the USS *Gerald Ford*, cost $13 billion, according to an article by Courtney Mabeus, 'How the World's Greatest Aircraft Carrier Became a $13 Billion Fiasco' in *Popular Mechanics* magazine, 8 February 2022, popularmechanics. com/military/a38941815/how-the-uss-gerald-r-ford-became-a-dollar13-billion-fiasco/

Gross Domestic Product of Trinidad & Tobago sourced from the World Bank, datatopics.worldbank.org/world-development-indicators/

Unit 1

1 According to Errol Musk, quoted in an article by Graeme Raubenheimer and John Van Der Berg, 'Stern South African Childhood Fuelled Musk's Ambition, Says Father' in International Business Times, 6 January 22, ibtimes.com/ stern-south-african-childhood-fuelled-musks-ambition-says-father-3528124

2 According to Errol Musk, quoted in Vlismas, 2022

3 The code for Musk's 1984 computer game Blastar was republished in the colour plates section of *Elon Musk: How the Billionaire CEO of SpaceX and Tesla Is Shaping Our Future* by Ashlee Vance (Virgin Books, London, 2015). You can play Blastar online at blastar-1984.appspot.com/

4 Musk's rapid peeing was reported by engineer Kevin Brogan, quoted in Vance, 2015, p. 231

5 Quoted in Vance, 2015, p. 48

6 Vance, 2015, p. 64

7 Matt Durot, 'New Billionaires 2022: Rihanna, Peter Jackson And 234 Others Join The Ranks This Year' in *Forbes* magazine, 5 April 2022, forbes.com/sites/mattdurot/2022/04/05/

billionaires-2022-rihanna-peter-jackson-and-234-others-new-to-the-list-this-year/?sh=549141cf1770

8 Vance, 2015, p. 58

9 According to former SolarCity CEO Lyndon Rive, interviewed by Alison Van Diggelen for Fresh Dialogues on 23 April 2012, freshdialogues.com/2012/04/23/elon-musk-solarcity-how-does-he-contribute/

10 Road trip origin story widely quoted including in a *Guardian* profile by Rupert Neate, 'Amazon's Jeff Bezos: the man who wants you to buy everything from his company', 22 June 2014, theguardian.com/theobserver/2014/jun/22/jeff-bezos-amazon-boss-wants-to-sell-you-everything

11 Vance, 2015, p. 58

12 Vance, 2015, p. 63

13 All-night coding sessions at Facebook described in 'Hacking All Night to an IPO' by Julia Boorstin, CNBC, 18 May 2012, cnbc.com/id/47474828

14 Mike Wall, 'Elon Musk Names SpaceX Drone Ships in Honor of Sci-Fi Legend' on space.com, 4 February 2015, space.com/28445-spacex-elon-musk-drone-ships-names.html

15 Vance, 2015, p. 59

16 Shatner's space flight at the age of ninety was reported widely including in an article by Richard Luscombe, 'William Shatner in tears after historic space flight: "I'm so filled with emotion"', *Guardian*, 13 October 2021, theguardian.com/science/2021/oct/13/william-shatner-jeff-bezos-rocket-blue-origin

17 Neal Stephenson's role at Blue Origin is mentioned in *Amazon Unbound* by Brad Stone (Simon & Schuster, London, 2021, p. 267)

18 According to an executive quoted in an article by Charles Duhigg, 'Dr Elon and Mr Musk: Inside Tesla's Production Hell' in *Wired*, 13 December 2018

19 Vance, 2015, p. 232

20 Vance, 2015, p. 240

21 Musk's penchant for unrealistic deadline setting is discussed on p. 233 of Vance, 2015

22 Elon Musk quoted by Justine Musk in her article 'I Was a Starter Wife:

Inside America's Messiest Divorce' in *Marie Claire*, 10 September 2010, marieclaire.com/sex-love/a5380/millionaire-starter-wife/

23 Senior Tesla employees quoted in *Power Play: Tesla, Elon Musk, and the Bet of the Century* by Tim Higgins (W.H. Allen, London, 2018), and in an article by Tim Higgins, 'Elon Musk faces his own worst enemy' in the *Wall Street Journal*, 31 August 2018, wsj.com/articles/elon-musk-faces-his-own-worst-enemy-1535727324

24 Vance, 2015, pp. 78–9

25 Vance, 2015, p. 80

Unit 2

1 Figures from article by Alyssa Pagano and Irene Anna Kim, 'How Tesla CEO Elon Musk makes and spends his $19.2 billion' in Business Insider, 24 June 2019, businessinsider.com/tesla-elon-musk-ceo-net-worth-makes-spends-billion-money-2019-6

2 Interview with Jeff Bezos in 1997, filmed at the Special Libraries (SLA) conference in Seattle, WA, youtube.com/watch?v=rWRbT-nE1PEM

3 Musk quoted in an interview by Carl Hoffman, 'Now 0-for-3, SpaceX's Elon Musk Vows to Make Orbit' in *Wired*, 5 August 2008, wired.com/2008/08/musk-qa/

4 Bezos quoted in an interview with John Stofflet for KING-TVs *Evening Magazine* in 2000, and referenced in an article by Taylor Locke on CNBC, 3 September 2020, cnbc.com/2020/09/03/jeff-bezos-thought-there-was-a-30percent-chance-amazon-would-succeed.html

5 Higgins, 2021, p. 226

6 Musk's denial was quoted by in an article by Nick Taylor, 'Elon Musk Denies He Discussed Apple-Tesla Merger With Tim Cook' on Bloomberg, 30 July 2021, bloomberg.com/news/articles/2021-07-30/musk-slams-apple-fees-and-denies-he-discussed-merger-with-cook

7 Vance, 2015, p. 100

8 Vance, 2015, p. 107

9 Number of Starlink satellites reported in article by Stephen Clark

for Spaceflight Now, 13 May 2022, spaceflightnow.com/2022/05/13/
spacex-passes-2500-satellites-launched-for-companys-starlink-
network/

10 Article by Jamie Carter, 'SpaceX's Starlink Satellites Could
Eventually Make Us Visible To Aliens Says Scientist',
in *Forbes* magazine, 18 March 2021, forbes.com/sites/
jamiecartereurope/2021/03/18/spacexs-starlink-satellites-could-
eventually-make-us-visible-to-aliens-says-scientist

11 China's complaint about Starlink near misses was reported in
'Elon Musk criticised after China space complaint to UN', BBC
News, 28 December 2021, bbc.co.uk/news/business-59806499

12 Vance, 2015, p. 284

13 Detailed in article by Peter Valdez-Dapena, 'Elon Musk explains
why the Cybertruck's windows broke' in CNN Business, 26
November 2019, edition.cnn.com/2019/11/25/cars/elon-musk-
tesla-cybertruck-window-glass-broke/index.html

14 Bethany McLean, 'How Elon Musk Fooled Investors, Bilked
Taxpayers, And Gambled Tesla To Save SolarCity', *Vanity Fair*,
25 August 2019, vanityfair.com/news/2019/08/how-elon-musk-
gambled-tesla-to-save-solarcity

15 Albuquerque lawsuit reported by Tony Ho Tran, 'Tesla Owners
Furious That Elon Musk Keeps Pushing Back Full Self-Driving'.
The Byte, 17 September 2021, futurism.com/the-byte/tesla-owners-
furious

   Munich court ruling reported by Lora Kolodny and Sam Shead,
'German court rules that Tesla misled consumers on Autopilot
and Full Self Driving' on CNBC, 14 July 2020

16 Yearly predictions of full self-driving shown on supercut video as
part of article by Victor Tangermann, 'Watch Elon Musk Promise
Self-Driving Cars "Next Year"', futurism.com/video-elon-musk-
promising-self-driving-cars

17 Report of Tesla crashing into a plane in Cody Godwin, 'Self-driving
Tesla crashes into $3.5 million private jet using "smart summon"
feature' in USA Today, 25 April 2022, eu.usatoday.com/videos/
news/have-you-seen/2022/04/25/tesla-collides-private-jet-while-
owner-using-smart-summon-mode/7439216001/

   Increase in phantom braking reported by Veronica Irwin, '107 drivers recently complained about their Teslas making random, jolting stops' in Protocol, 2 February 2022, protocol.com/bulletins/tesla-phantom-braking

18 Article by Daniel Muoio, 'Elon Musk: Tesla's factory will be an "alien dreadnought" by 2018' in Business Insider, 27 October 2016, businessinsider.com/elon-musk-tesla-factory-alien-dreadnought-2016-10?r=US&IR=T

19 As per claims on SpaceX website, spacex.com/human-spaceflight/earth/index.html

20 Bezos's slogan, 'It's always day one', discussed in an article by Ram Charan and Julia Yang, 'Jeff Bezos' philosophy for Amazon is that it's always "Day 1" – here's what that means and why it works', in Business Insider, 10 December 2019

21 Blog article by Musk, 'The Secret Tesla Motors Master Plan (just between you and me)', 2 August 2006, tesla.com/blog/secret-tesla-motors-master-plan-just-between-you-and-me

22 Tweet about going interstellar, 24 November 2021, twitter.com/elonmusk/status/1463562289643151360

23 An account of the Sun Valley, Idaho, billionaire summer camp is given in an article by Benjamin Mullin, 'When Private Jets Ferry Billionaires to Small-Town Idaho' in the New York Times, 1 July 2022, nytimes.com/2022/07/01/business/sun-valley-conference-private-jets.html

24 Warren Buffett is quoted talking about 'elephant bumping' in an article by Alice Schroeder, 'Warren Buffett: Billionaire's tell-all bio' in People magazine, 26 September 2008, today.com/popculture/warren-buffett-billionaire-s-tell-all-bio-wbna26888245

25 Article by Alexia Fernández Campbell, 'Elon Musk broke US labor laws on Twitter' in Vox, 30 September 2019, vox.com/identities/2019/9/30/20891314/elon-musk-tesla-labor-violation-nlrb

26 Reported in an article by Jason Del Rey, 'America finally gets an Amazon union' in Vox, 1 April 2022, vox.com/recode/23005336/amazon-union-new-york-warehouse

27 Article by Laura Kolodny, 'Tesla monitored its employees on Facebook with help of PR firm during 2017 union push' on CNBC, 2 June 2022, cnbc.com/2022/06/02/tesla-paid-pr-firm-to-surveil-employees-on-facebook-in-2017-union-push.html

Unit 3

1 Vance, 2015, p. 76

2 The Sultan of Brunei's exhaustingly large car collection is detailed in an article by Lynn Farah, 'How the Sultan of Brunei Hassanal Bolkiah spends his billions: gold Rolls-Royces, a gilded Boeing 747, US$70 million works of art by Renoir and the biggest residential palace in the world' in the *South China Morning Post*, 16 April 22, scmp.com/magazines/style/celebrity/article/3174250/how-sultan-brunei-hassanal-bolkiah-spends-his-billions

3 Account of the origins of The Boring Company, Vlismas, 2022, p. 205

4 250 flights in a year reported by Drew Harwell, 'Elon Musk's highflying 2018: What 150,000 miles in a private jet reveal about his excruciating year' in the *Washington Post*, 29 January 2019, washingtonpost.com/business/economy/elon-musks-highflying-2018-what-150000-miles-in-a-private-jet-reveal-about-his-excruciating-year/2019/01/29/83b5604e-20ee-11e9-8b59-0a28f2191131_story.html

   Nine-minute flight reported in 'Elon Musk's 9-minute Flight Sparks Discussion on Carbon Footprint of the Super Rich' on News 18, 8 May 2022, news18.com/news/buzz/elon-musks-9-minute-flight-sparks-discussion-on-carbon-footprint-of-the-super-rich-5134225.html

5 Musk's glamorous Bel Air life is described in Vance, 2015, p. 183

6 Reported in article by Chris White, 'EXCLUSIVE: Mark Zuckerberg's $37M 'five-house estate' in Palo Alto is seen in aerial photos for the first time after years of battles with neighbours over compound' in the *Daily Mail*, 17 December 2021, dailymail.co.uk/news/article-10314439/Mark-Zuckerbergs-37M-five-house-estate-Palo-Alto-seen-aerial-photos.htmlZuckerberg buying surrounding mansions

7 Reported in article by Stuart Dredge, 'Tesla founder Elon Musk buys James Bond's Lotus Esprit submarine car', *Guardian*, 18 October 2013, theguardian.com/technology/2013/oct/18/tesla-elon-musk-james-bond-lotus-submarine-car

8 10,000-year clock detailed on project website, 'The Clock of the Long Now', longnow.org/clock/

9 Mukesh Ambani's Antilia residence is detailed in an article by Vrushali Padia, 'Inside Antilia: The World's Most Expensive Private Residence' on TheRichest.com, 3 October 2021, therichest.com/luxury-architecture/inside-antilia-the-worlds-most-expensive-private-residence/

10 Article by Bernadette Deron, 'Titanic 2 Plans To Complete Its Namesake's Doomed Journey In 2022' in All That's Interesting, 20 September 2021, allthatsinteresting.com/titanic-2-ship

11 Larry Ellison's fighter jets are described in an article by Paige Leskin, 'From Elon Musk to Bill Gates, here are all of the notable tech billionaires who jet around the world in private planes' on Business Insider, 17 June 2019, businessinsider.com/private-planes-jets-tech-billionaires-2019-3?r=US&IR=T#oracle-founder-larry-ellison-is-known-for-his-opulent-nature-and-oft-unusual-behavior-ellison-is-an-avid-sailor-and-a-licensed-pilot-his-son-david-is-a-stunt-pilot-who-has-been-flying-with-his-dad-since-he-was-13-10

12 The story of Steve Cohen's pig is reported in an article by Julia La Roche, 'Turns out hedge fund billionaire Steve Cohen DID have a large pig living in his Connecticut mansion' in Business Insider, 10 June 2015, businessinsider.com/steve-cohen-did-have-a-pig-2015-6?r=US&IR=T

13 Sheikh Hamad bin Hamdan Al Nahyan's giant graffiti tag in the sand is reported in an article by Christopher Helman, 'Abu Dhabi Oil Sheikh Writes His Name In The Sand, Two Miles Wide' in *Forbes*, 20 July 2011, forbes.com/sites/christopherhelman/2011/07/20/abu-dhabi-oil-sheikh-writes-his-name-in-the-sand-two-miles-wide/?sh=384a78157057

14 Launch of Floki Inu currency detailed by Sian Bradley, 'Floki Inu coin price and what is the cryptocurrency?' on Chronicle Live, 1 November 2021, chroniclelive.co.uk/business/floki-inu-coin-price-what-22033680

15 Article by Hayley Glatter, 'Jeff Bezos Walked with a Boston Dynamics SpotMini Robot' in the *Boston Magazine*, 21 March 2018, bostonmagazine.com/news/2018/03/21/jeff-bezos-boston-dynamics-dog/

16 Altos Labs, the life extension start-up Bezos has invested in, is

discussed in an article by Caroline Delbert, 'Jeff Bezos Is Paying For a Way to Make Humans Immortal' in *Popular Mechanics* magazine, 26 January 2022, popularmechanics.com/technology/startups/a38867242/jeff-bezos-altos-labs/

17 Advent of armed robot dogs is reported by James Vincent in 'They're putting guns on robot dogs now', in The Verge, 14 October 2021, theverge.com/2021/10/14/22726111/robot-dogs-with-guns-sword-international-ghost-robotics

18 Tweet by Elon Musk, 1 May 2020, twitter.com/elonmusk/status/1256239554148724737

19 Reported in an article by Rob Copeland, 'Elon Musk Says He Lives in a $50,000 House. He Doesn't Talk About the Austin Mansion' in the *Wall Street Journal*, 22 December 2021, wsj.com/articles/elon-musk-says-he-lives-in-a-50-000-house-he-doesnt-talk-about-the-austin-mansion-11640188548

20 Reported in feature by Devin Gordon, '"Infamy Is Kind Of Fun": Grimes on Music, Mars, and Her Secret New Baby With Elon Musk' in *Vanity Fair*, 10 March 2022, vanityfair.com/style/2022/03/grimes-cover-story-on-music-and-mars

21 Article by Sissi Cao, 'Elon Musk's $50,000 Box Home Exists, But, Surprise, He Kinda Lives in a Billionaire Friend's Mansion' in *Observer*, 23 December 2021, observer.com/2021/12/elon-musk-staying-at-billionaire-friends-mansion/

22 Reported in an article by Tim Levin, 'Elon Musk, once again the world's richest person, is selling all his possessions so people know he's serious about colonizing Mars', in Business Insider, 19 February 2021, businessinsider.in/thelife/news/elon-musk-now-the-worlds-richest-person-is-selling-all-his-possessions-so-people-know-hes-serious-about-colonizing-mars/articleshow/80162190.cms

23 From an Ashlee Vance interview with Larry Page, quoted in an article by Jillian Donfro, 'Google CEO Larry Page says Elon Musk is "kind of homeless" in Silicon Valley and sometimes asks if he can sleep over', Business Insider, 11 May 2015, businessinsider.in/Google-CEO-Larry-Page-says-Elon-Musk-is-kind-of-homeless-in-Silicon-Valley-and-sometimes-asks-if-he-can-sleep-over/articleshow/47237147.cms

24 Tweet by Elon Musk, 27 May 2022, twitter.com/elonmusk/status/1529961091656212514

25 Musk quoted in article 'Tesla's Musk says Biden's EV bill shouldn't pass', on Reuters wire, 7 December 2021, reuters.com/article/tesla-biden-ev-idCNL4N2SS0IQ

26 Article by Maggie Severns, Matt Stiles and Alex Leeds, 'Elon Musk hates government subsidies. His companies love them' in *Grid* magazine, 30 April 2022, grid.news/story/technology/2022/04/30/elon-musk-hates-the-government-his-companies-love-it/

27 Figures from ProPublica research by Jesse Eisinger, Jeff Ernsthausen and Paul Kiel, 'The Secret IRS Files: Trove of Never-Before-Seen Records Reveal How the Wealthiest Avoid Income Tax', 8 June 2021, propublica.org/article/the-secret-irs-files-trove-of-never-before-seen-records-reveal-how-the-wealthiest-avoid-income-tax

28 According to an an article by Joe Light and Ben Stupples, 'A $6 trillion family office world fights post-Archegos crackdown', in Bloomberg, 18 May 2021, family offices serving a single family and with no outside clients generally don't need to register with the SEC as investment advisers. bloomberg.com/professional/blog/a--6-trillion-family-office-world-fights-post-archegos-crackdown/

29 Family offices control $6–7 trillion, compared to $3.4 trillion controlled by hedge funds, according to a briefing paper by Chuck Collins and Kalena Thomhave, 'Family Offices: A Vestige of the Shadow Financial System' for the Institute for Policy Studies, https://inequality.org/wp-content/uploads/2021/05/Primer-FamilyOffices-May24-2021.pdf

30 Bill Gates' family office, run by Michael Larson, and his previous money manager Andrew Evans, who served six months for bank fraud, are discussed in an article by Anupreeta Das, Emily Flitter and Nicholas Kulish, 'A Culture of Fear at the Firm That Manages Bill Gates's Fortune', in the *New York Times*, 26 May 2021, nytimes.com/2021/05/26/business/bill-gates-cascade-michael-larson.html

31 Article by Hayley Cuccinello, 'Meet Jared Birchall, the secretive man that Elon Musk trusts with his billions' in Business Insider, 4 July 2022, businessinsider.com/meet-elon-musk-money-manager-jared-birchall?r=US&IR=T

32 Article by Leslie Albrecht, 'The Giving Pledge turns 10: These billion-aires pledged to give away half their wealth, but they soon ran into a problem' in Market Watch, 10 August 2020, marketwatch.com/story/giving-away-money-well-is-very-hard-the-giving-pledge-turns-10-and-its-signers-are-richer-than-ever-2020-08-08

Unit 4

1 Reported in article by Tom Huddleston Jr, 'Elon Musk: CEO is a "made-up title," so he's Tesla's "Technoking" instead' on CNBC, 7 December 2021, cnbc.com/2021/12/07/elon-musk-ceo-is-made-up-title-prefers-tesla-technoking.html
2 Taken from Statista research, 'General Motors Company's adver-tising spending worldwide from 2015 to 2021', statista.com/statistics/286522/general-motors-advertising-spending-worldwide/
3 Musk's friendship with Pranay Pathole is described in an article by Omaire Pall, 'Who Is Pranay Pathole? The Pune Engineer Who Is Elon Musk's Twitter Buddy' on Mashable, 15 March 2022, in.mashable.com/culture/28729/who-is-pranay-pathole-the-pune-engineer-who-is-elon-musks-twitter-buddy
4 Story described in an article by Sean O'Kane, 'The lesson from Elon Musk's "funding secured" mess is to never tweet' on the Verge, 7 August 2019, https://www.theverge.com/tldr/2019/8/7/20758944/elon-musk-twitter-tesla-funding-secured-private-420
5 Article by Samantha Subin, 'Elon Musk offers to buy Twitter for $43 billion, so it can be "transformed as private company"' on CNBC, 14 April 2022, cnbc.com/2022/04/14/elon-musk-offers-to-buy-twitter-for-54point20-a-share-saying-it-needs-to-be-transformed-as-private-company.html
6 Tweet by Elon Musk, 14 October 2020 twitter.com/elonmusk/status/1316454051693895680?s=20&t=sue0Juz3LI8lvtoyJl_jHA
7 Article by Christopher Hooks, 'Elon Musk Is Turning Boca Chica Into a Space-Travel Hub. Not Everyone Is Starstruck' in Texas Monthly, June 2021, texasmonthly.com/news-politics/elon-musk-boca-chica-starbase-texas/
8 The search for Amazon's new HQ is detailed in Brad Stone, 2021, chapter 12, including Amazon's initial choice of both New York

City and Northern Virginia. Eventually negative public opinion scuppered the New York plans.

9 Article by Hyunjoo Jin and Sheila Dang, 'Musk says U.S. SEC "bastards" forced settlement over Tesla tweets' on Reuters, 14 April 2022, reuters.com/technology/musk-says-us-sec-bastards-forced-settlement-over-tesla-tweets-2022-04-14/

10 Ibid.

11 These and more insults are catalogued in an article by Bess Levin in *Vanity Fair*, 'A Reminder of Just Some of the Terrible Things Elon Musk Has Said and Done', 26 April 2022, vanityfair.com/news/2022/04/elon-musk-twitter-terrible-things-hes-said-and-done

12 JDART tactics described in Vlismas, 2022, p. 187–8

13 Tweet by Elon Musk, 31 May 2022, twitter.com/elonmusk/status/1531647849599057921?s=20&t=jJWNksvtKVUcnyIU-f24aQ

14 Tweets by Elon Musk, 1 June 2022, twitter.com/elonmusk/status/1532028817157591041?s=20&t=8xWMSmUm532sebLe3opCtg

15 Parties involved in bid coalition reported in an article by Adam Smith, 'Elon Musk's Twitter backers suggest a big fight for the future of the social network' in the Independent, 6 May 2022, independent.co.uk/tech/elon-musk-twitter-free-speech-b2073024.html

16 Failure to criticise China's lockdown policies were noted in an article by Jane Li, 'Elon Musk railed against US covid controls – but not Shanghai's lockdown', in Quartz, 19 April 2022, qz.com/2156327/elon-musk-railed-against-us-covid-controls-but-not-shanghai-lockdown/

   'Give people back their goddamn freedom' was from an earnings call in April 2020, as reported in an article by Lauren Hepler and David Pierce, 'Elon Musk's COVID-19 meltdown: "Give people back their goddamn freedom"', in Protocol, 29 April 2020, protocol.com/elon-musk-derails-tesla-earnings-call

17 The Lawrence Fossi case was reported in an article by Michael Luciano, '"Extreme Enemy of Free Speech": Tesla Critic Says Elon Musk Bullied Him Off Twitter in 2018 By Calling His Boss and Threatening to Sue' in Mediaite, 26 April 2022, mediaite.com/tech/lawrence-fossi-speaks-out-on-elon-musk/

   The rude customer having their order cancelled was reported

in article by Arjun Kharpal, 'Musk denies "super-rude" client his Tesla' on CNBC, 3 February 2016, cnbc.com/2016/02/03/elon-musk-personally-cancels-rude-customers-tesla-order.html

18 Employee NDAs were reported in an article by Lora Kolodny, 'Elon Musk says he wants free speech, but his track record suggests otherwise' on CNBC, 25 April 2022, cnbc.com/2022/04/25/elon-musk-and-free-speech-track-record-not-encouraging.html

Termination of contracts for employees who wrote a letter criticising his Twitter usage was reported in an article by Christiaan Hetzner, 'SpaceX has reportedly fired the employees behind the letter denouncing Elon Musk's "embarrassing" behavior' in Fortune magazine, 17 June 2022, fortune.com/2022/06/17/spacex-elon-musk-employee-letter-staff-fired-sacked-terminations

19 Vance, 2015, p. 221

20 Musk announced he was voting Republican in a tweet on 18 May 2022: 'In the past I voted Democrat, because they were (mostly) the kindness party. But they have become the party of division & hate, so I can no longer support them and will vote Republican', twitter.com/elonmusk/status/1526997132858822658

21 From a tweet by Musk, 15 July 2022, twitter.com/elonmusk/status/1547927887734456322

22 Musk talks frequently about preserving or extending 'the light of consciousness', for example in a tweet on 25 June 2018, twitter.com/elonmusk/status/1011083630301536256

23 The WeWork story has been told by many, including Lauren Feiner, 'WeWork offers a romantic vision in its IPO filing – alongside staggering losses', on CNBC, 19 August 2019, and dramatised in the miniseries *WeCrashed*, cnbc.com/2019/08/14/wework-ipo-filing-sells-a-romantic-vision-alongside-losses.html

Unit 5

1 Quoted in an article by Matt McFarland, 'Elon Musk: "With artificial intelligence we are summoning the demon"', in the *Washington Post*, 24 October 2014, washingtonpost.com/news/innovations/wp/2014/10/24/elon-musk-with-artificial-intelligence-we-are-summoning-the-demon/

2 Quoted in an article by Margo Oge, 'Where Does Elon Musk Really Stand on Fighting Climate Change?' in *Forbes* magazine, 17 January 2022, forbes.com/sites/margooge/2022/01/17/where-does-elon-musk-really-stand-on-fighting-climate-change

3 Quoted in an article by Thomas Barrabi, 'Elon Musk reveals 3 biggest existential threats to humanity's survival' in the *New York Post*, 28 March 2022, nypost.com/2022/03/28/elon-musk-reveals-3-biggest-existential-threats-to-humanitys-survival/

4 Ibid.

5 From a Twitter exchange with Pranay Pathole quoted in an article by Jeff Parsons, 'Elon Musk blames "the woke mind virus" for people deserting Netflix', 20 April 2022, metro.co.uk/2022/04/20/elon-musk-blames-woke-mind-virus-for-making-netflix-unwatchable-16502140/

6 Quoted in an article by Richard Waters and Hannah Murphy, 'Elon Musk fails to convince the doubters that he will "save" Twitter' in the *Financial Times*, 16 April 2022, ft.com/content/bdaa0a37-9f4f-4bcc-8f3a-ca9261186e8c

7 LinkedIn founder Reid Hoffman says that half of billionaires have some kind of 'apocalypse insurance' measures in an article by Evan Osnos, 'Doomsday Prep for the Super Rich', in the *New Yorker*, 30 January 2017, newyorker.com/magazine/2017/01/30/doomsday-prep-for-the-super-rich

8 Article by Graeme Massie, 'Jeff Bezos predicts people will one day be born in space and "visit Earth the way you visit Yellowstone National Park"', *Independent*, 12 November 2021, independent.co.uk/space/bezos-space-colonies-earth-tourism-b1956834.html

9 Quoted in an article by Aric Jenkins, 'How Elon Musk Plans to Create a "Self-Sustaining City" on Mars' in Fortune and Yahoo Finance, 15 June 2017, uk.finance.yahoo.com/news/elon-musk-plans-create-apos-200255780.html

10 Quoted in an article by Tom McKay, 'Elon Musk: A New Life Awaits You in the Off-World Colonies – for a Price', 17 January 2020, gizmodo.com/elon-musk-a-new-life-awaits-you-on-the-off-world-colon-1841071257

11 Elon Musk interview on Clubhouse, 7 February 2021, zamesin.ru/ clubhouse-elon-musk-interview/

12 Article by Hannah Ryan in CNN Business, 'Elon Musk's Neuralink confirms monkeys died in project, denies animal cruelty claims', 17 February 2022, edition.cnn.com/2022/02/17/business/elon-musk-neuralink-animal-cruelty-intl-scli/index.html

13 Tweet by Elon Musk, 6 June 2022, twitter.com/elonmusk/ status/1533600925209837568

14 The Future of Humanity Institute at Oxford University receives funding from Musk, as reported on its website on 1 July 2015, fhi.ox.ac.uk/elon-musk-funds-oxford-and-cambridge-university-research-on-safe-and-beneficial-artificial-intelligence/

15 Quoted in an article by Catherine Clifford, 'Jeff Bezos dreams of a world with a trillion people living in space' on CNBC, 1 May 2018, cnbc.com/2018/05/01/jeff-bezos-dreams-of-a-world-with-a-trillion-people-living-in-space.html

16 Reported in an article by Anthony Cuthbertson, 'Elon Musk cites Pong as evidence that we are already living in a simulation' in the *Independent*, 1 December 2021, independent.co.uk/space/elon-musk-simulation-pong-video-game-b1972369.html

17 'Player of Games' is the title of a single by Grimes, presumed to be about Musk, youtube.com/watch?v=ADHFwabVJec